THE OUTBREAK
OF THE SECOND WORLD WAR

Design or Blunder?

PROBLEMS IN EUROPEAN CIVILIZATION

UNDER THE EDITORIAL DIRECTION OF

Ralph W. Greenlaw* and Dwight E. Lee†

Other volumes in preparation

PROBLEMS IN EUROPEAN CIVILIZATION

THE OUTBREAK
OF THE
SECOND WORLD WAR

Design or Blunder?

EDITED WITH AN INTRODUCTION BY

John L. Snell, TULANE UNIVERSITY

D. C. HEATH AND COMPANY · BOSTON

Table of Contents

Introduction

EARLY in 1946 the "Cold War" was openly acknowledged by Stalin and Churchill in two famous speeches. Both offered brief — and highly divergent — explanations of the causes of the Second World War.

Stalin's explanation, as given over Radio Moscow on February 9, 1946, provided guidelines for future Soviet historians:

It would be incorrect to think that the war arose accidentally or as the result of the fault of some of the statesmen. Although these faults did exist, the war arose in reality as the *inevitable* result of the development of the world economic and political forces on the basis of monopoly capitalism. [Italics added.]

Stalin thus reverted to an old theme of Lenin's that had been repressed during the war against Germany when the "strange alliance" with the West was necessary. Stalin's revival of this argument in 1946 put the West on notice that the U.S.S.R. would prepare for the possibility of another major war.

Churchill spoke soon thereafter at Fulton, Missouri, on March 5, 1946. His view of the causes of World War II had always put primary guilt on Nazi Germany. But at Fulton — as for years before — he also assigned a large responsibility to the appeasement policy of Germany's neighbors in the 1930's:

There never was a war in all history easier to prevent by timely action than the one which has just desolated such great areas of the globe. It could have been prevented without the firing of a single shot . . . but no one would listen and one by one we were all sucked into the awful whirlpool. We surely must not let that happen again.

Quite clearly, Churchill, no less than Stalin, was drawing lessons for 1946 from his view of the causes of World War II. Refusing to agree that capitalism — or anything else — made war *inevitable*, Churchill was saying that softness invites aggression; and indirectly he was saying that firmness toward the U.S.S.R. could prevent a third World War, just as firmness toward Nazi Germany could have prevented World War II.

The policies of nations have often been shaped — or justified — by views of the past, but seldom so strikingly as in the exchange of 1946, just reviewed. With their eyes on the thirties, the two statesmen drew conclusions about the needs of the 1940's, and their conclusions profoundly shaped the fate of people in the East and the West in the fifties and sixties.

The speeches of Stalin and Churchill suggest questions that are posed for you in this book. Did the Second World War come as a result of design? Whose design? Or was it the result of blunder? Whose blunder? These are questions of great historical importance, for the war that began in 1939 was the greatest in history. But they are more than questions of historical interest. Answers to them have great relevance to the present. What we think about the causes of the Second World War will be in considerable measure an augury of our future.

Our view of the past formidably influences our present and our future. But just as surely the conditions of our present — and sometimes what we want out of the future — influence the view we hold of the past. Because of ever-recurring new "presents," new angles of vision from which we view the past, historical interpretations of major events change. The discovery of new knowledge also changes interpretations of historical events. Thus, even in the relatively short period since 1939 many shifts in emphasis have occurred in explanations of the outbreak of World War II.

The first interpretations of the causes of a war are always offered before the fighting begins by contemporaries who — by luck or wisdom — see it coming. The first *historical* interpretations can be presented only after war begins. They were freely given during the war of 1939–1945, as they have been in every major war in history. These wartime views have often powerfully shaped future historical interpretations, because they gain widespread currency. True or false, they become legends — popular history that tends to be clung to by the masses of people long after scholars revise their opinions.

The view of the causes of World War II accepted in wartime by most of the peoples of the world was that view set forth by their national leaders in propaganda speeches to build fighting spirit. It requires little imagination to sense that this view varied widely in Poland and Germany, in Great Britain and Italy, in France, the United States, the Soviet Union, and elsewhere. These views had only one thing in common: each nation's leaders argued that the war came as a result of design by the evil statesmen of the enemy nations.

Historians in wartime developed more complex and more accurate explanations for the educated reading public. An excellent example of wartime historical scholarship, applied to the very recent past, was provided by Dwight E. Lee in 1942 in *Ten Years: The World on the Way to War, 1930–1940.*[1] This book was read by a great many American college students during and just after World War II. With a balance that today may seem surprising, Lee's account acknowledged the existence

of both design and blunder among the causes of the Second World War. Responsibility was not exclusively placed on a single nation, though Germany's primary guilt was clearly affirmed. Western appeasement of Nazi Germany was criticized, as was Soviet appeasement in 1939. A student who wants to see how well history can be written close to the event, amidst wartime passions and with most of the documents still unpublished, can consult the Lee volume with profit.

Documents that Lee could not study in 1941 were available by the tons to the International Military Tribunal that tried Nazi war criminals at Nuremberg in 1945–1946. The temper that then prevailed differed from that of 1941 and from the temper the Cold War soon created. The judges at Nuremberg wrote history as well as a legal judgment; indeed, they based their legal judgment squarely on the history they wrote. Their view of history, as they themselves stated it in their legal judgment, is presented in the first reading in this book. Victory's verdict at Nuremberg held that Germany's Nazi leaders had very deliberately — by design — prepared and started the Second World War. Germany's leaders were exclusively blamed for the war.

How was the Nuremberg verdict affected by the fact that no Germans were among the judges? By the fact that Italians and Poles were not present as either judges or accused? By the fact that the Soviet Union was represented among the prosecution and the judges? By the fact that Great Britain, France, and the United States made up — with the U.S.S.R. — the prosecution and the judges?

Many of the factors that influenced the Nuremberg view of history were altered by 1947. The "Cold War" had then broken the wartime spirit of solidarity among the four great powers that at Nuremberg had rendered a common judgment of German leaders and history. In 1948 the United States Department of State published a collection of German documents that had

[1] For publication data of all books mentioned in this introduction, see "Suggestions for Additional Reading," page 104.

been captured at the end of the war: *Nazi-Soviet Relations, 1939–1941*. These documents had not been used at Nuremberg. They were published in 1948 to score a propaganda victory for the West in the Cold War, and this they did. By showing how the Soviet Union had entered into the pact of August 23, 1939, with Hitler's Germany, they provided a basis for the first major post-Nuremberg revision of interpretations of the outbreak of World War II. The conclusion these documents yielded had been seldom drawn during the years of common struggle against Hitler. Since their publication, many historians have treated the Nazi-Soviet pact of August 23, 1939, as a "green light" for Hitler to drive into Poland on September 1. Was this agreement comparable to the "blank check" that Germany gave Austria-Hungary in 1914 against Serbia? The "blank check" of 1914 had been cited afterward as proof of Germany's guilt for World War I; with similar logic, it could be argued that the U.S.S.R. was responsible for World War II.

Was Soviet action on August 23, 1939, the product of design or blunder? According to one western expert on Soviet affairs, Stalin's action in 1939 was not a sudden act of either opportunism or desperation, but one long premeditated. Even in 1936–1937, during the heyday of the Popular Front, writes Leonard Schapiro, Stalin did not "abandon his endeavors, now conducted in the greatest secrecy, to pursue his original plan of an alliance with Hitler."[2] The negotiations the Soviets conducted in 1939 with both Germany and the western democracies are described in some detail in the second reading by William L. Langer and S. Everett Gleason, who based their account upon the documents published in 1948 by the Department of State and other material available by 1952.

But the Soviet Union had also captured German documents at the end of World War II, and in 1948 it had its own propagandists ready to counterattack in the Cold War ideological-historical contest. Its documents, like the documents the United States published in 1948, had not been used at Nuremberg. They were released by the Ministry of Foreign Affairs of the U.S.S.R. under the title *Documents and Materials Relating to the Eve of the Second World War.* The State Department had let readers draw their own conclusions; the Soviet authorities left nothing to chance. The Soviet Information Bureau released in advance of the documents a brochure entitled *Falsificators of History.* Both documents and brochure attempted to show that British and French leaders in the 1930's had — by design rather than blunder — appeased Hitler's ambitious foreign policy demands. The Soviet publications pointed up the fact that the U.S.S.R., before entering the pact with Hitler, had proclaimed its desire for collective security against him. The Soviet publications were designed to prove that Hitler went to war in 1939 because he was convinced that the western capitalist democracies would not stop him — even encouraged him — in a drive to the East in the direction of the U.S.S.R. Thus the Soviet Union tried to prove that the West, not the U.S.S.R., had obstructed the formation of a common front against the dictators in 1939; that the "green light" or the "blank check" of 1939 had been given not by Stalin but by Chamberlain, Daladier, and Roosevelt.

This view has not been widely accepted in the West, although it is basically accepted by D. F. Fleming in *The Cold War and Its Origins, 1917–1960* (pp. 86–97). It is treated as absolute truth in the U.S.S.R. The following quotation, taken from a history textbook used in Soviet secondary schools after 1948, shows the interpretation the U.S.S.R. gave of its action in 1939:

Taking into account the growing danger of the outbreak of another world war and the direct menace of an attack upon the U.S.S.R., the Soviet government opened negotiations with the representatives of Great Britain and France for the conclusion of a pact of mutual assistance against fascist aggression in Europe; but these negotiations failed owing to the intrigues of the extreme reactionary circles in those countries who were hostile to the U.S.S.R., and who wanted, by striking a bargain with fascist Germany, to turn the latter's aggression exclusively against the Soviet Union.

Meanwhile, the German government offered to conclude a pact of non-aggression with the U.S.S.R. This pact established a basis for enduring peace between the two biggest states in Europe, . . . The wise foreign policy pursued by the Soviet government . . . raised its prestige in the eyes of the working people all over the world.[3]

These themes are developed at length in the third reading, which is taken from the Soviet publication *Falsificators of History*. There you will find the Soviet argument that the United States spurred on the British and French encouragement of Nazi aggression against the Soviet Union. The Soviet view of 1948 only hardened during the decade that followed. How valid is it? When you have read all the accounts in this book you must decide, at least tentatively, for yourself who the real "falsificators of history" have been, and whether it was by design or blunder that a common front against Hitler was not formed in 1939.

Soviet propaganda has not been the only source of accusations that the United States was partly responsible for the outbreak of war in 1939. The complaint has come from the American Right as well as from the Communist Left. In 1952 (an election year) an American historian, Charles Callan Tansill, published a large book in which he argued that President Franklin D. Roosevelt played a significant part in the outbreak of war in 1939 by encouraging Poland, Britain, and France to

[3] A. M. Pankratova, ed., *A History of the U.S.S.R.*, 3 vols. (Moscow, 1947–1948), III, 387–388.

resist Hitler's demands. Published in translation, the Tansill book sold thousands of copies in Germany in the late 1950's, notwithstanding reviews by German historians that criticized its scholarship and its politics. An excerpt from the Tansill book, presenting the essence of its case against Roosevelt's role in the 1939 crisis, appears as the fourth reading. Is Tansill's thesis more acceptable than the contradictory Soviet assertions that United States policy encouraged Hitler to undertake an aggressive war? If both of these extreme interpretations are to be dismissed, can you think of any other reason why the United States should — in more modest degree — share responsibility for the outbreak of the war? It has been argued that the United States must share responsibility, because (contrary to the Tansill thesis) an isolationist foreign policy made it impossible for Roosevelt publicly to declare American support for Britain and France in their efforts to curb German expansion. On the other hand, the German ambassador in Washington after 1937 repeatedly advised Berlin that if war should come the United States would join Britain's side. Hitler seems to have ignored these warnings. Would he have ignored an open warning if Roosevelt had given one? Would a public declaration of support by Roosevelt have strengthened the British and French and caused them to abandon their efforts to appease Nazi Germany much earlier than they did? If so, would that have prevented the war, or hastened its coming?

While the Soviets and the American Right with opposite contentions blamed Roosevelt's policy for the breakdown of peace in 1939, the role of Poland in prewar diplomacy was being reexamined. No representatives of Poland were present at Nuremberg in either the prosecution or the defense. But since World War II began as a German-Polish war, Polish policies before the outbreak would inevitably be subjected to close scrutiny.

Hitler in 1939 justified his attack by insisting that the Polish government was treating Germans within Polish borders in an intolerable way and by telling the German people that the Poles had attacked Germany, not vice versa. This allegation was dismissed in the West during the war, and has not been seriously revived since. Thus most historians have tended to believe that the demands of 1939 were only pretexts for a war through which Hitler was determined to obtain much more than an auto highway and Danzig. As one German historian has put it: "Hitler did not begin this war for the sake of Danzig or the allegedly severely oppressed Germans in Poland. These things played . . . only a propagandistic role. . . . His aim was living space in the East."[4]

The idea that the war came by Polish design has been treated as unworthy of serious consideration. But what about Polish blunder? Is it possible that through the faults of its foreign policy Poland unwittingly contributed to the outbreak of the war? This question requires knowledge and appraisal of the policies of Colonel Józef Beck, who served as Poland's Minister of Foreign Affairs during the 1930's. The biggest count against him is that he obstructed the formation with the U.S.S.R. of a common front that might have curbed German aggression. Could Poland have entered such an alliance without losing independence and territory to the Soviet Union? Should even these sacrifices have been made to prevent the war? Both facts and interpretations are provided in the fifth reading by Henry L. Roberts.

In the great debate of 1948 Italy's partial responsibility for the outbreak of World War II was not emphasized. In 1943 the Italian government had saved Italy from the worst consequences of defeat by abandoning Germany and declaring war against her on the side of the Allies. By 1948 the West was ardently courting the new Italy as a partner against Communist expansion. The Soviet leaders on their part had hopes that Italian Communists would soon bring Italy into their camp. These new developments were already in progress in 1945–1946, and no Italians were brought to trial at Nuremberg. And yet troublesome memories remained in many minds. Mussolini had tolerated Hitler's annexation of Austria in March, 1938; he had helped Hitler achieve triumph at Munich in September, 1938; he had made the "pact of steel" of May 22, 1939, with Nazi Germany after Hitler had already used force to seize Prague and Memel in March, 1939; Mussolini himself had invaded Ethiopia in 1935 and Albania on Good Friday in April, 1939; his support for Nazi Germany in the "Rome-Berlin Axis" had been a major factor causing the British and French to hesitate so long before standing up to Hitler.

In Rome, as in Washington and Moscow, prewar documents were opened after World War II. In 1948, on the basis of these documents, a distinguished Italian historian, Mario Toscano, published an important volume on Fascist Italy's relations with Nazi Germany (*Le Origini del patto d'acciaio*). Toscano's book and the documents he quoted provide the basis for the sixth reading in this book. Written by a distinguished British historian, L. B. Namier, this essay should help you assess Italian responsibility for the coming of the war. Was it Italy rather than the U.S.S.R. that gave the "blank check" of 1939? Other readings in this book also throw light on this matter. Should Italy be assigned a major share of responsibility? To the extent that this has not been done, it represents a considerable revision of interpretation since the war years.

By the time you have studied the first six readings in this book it will be obvious that the Nuremberg judgment has been — implicitly if not explicitly — modified in different ways. Yet, whatever emphasis historians have given to the contributing responsibility of one nation or another, those

[4] Ludwig Denne, *Das Danzig-Problem in der deutschen Aussenpolitik 1934–1939* (Bonn, 1959), 293. See also Martin Broszat, *Nationalsozialistische Polenpolitik 1939–1945* (Stuttgart, 1961), 5–13.

who wrote the most impressive studies agreed — at least until 1961 — that Hitler's responsibility was unique. Within ten years after its end the publication of pre-war documents had caused historians to distribute responsibility for the war of 1914 among at least two or three nations; in contrast, as documents on the diplomacy of the 1930's became available in the decade after 1945 they only seemed to reinforce the belief that responsibility of the Nazi leaders for the outbreak of World War II was beyond question, almost beyond measure, and certainly beyond comparison with the secondary responsibility of other states.

By 1956, in addition to the Nuremberg records, the 1939 records of the Italian Foreign Ministry, the German Foreign Office, the British Foreign Ministry, and the United States Department of State had been published. In the seventh reading in this book — written on the basis of the documents available in 1956 — Raymond J. Sontag reviews the development of the Polish crisis in 1939. From Sontag's essay, Hitler's responsibility clearly emerged. Sontag in all essentials thus verified the 1954 interpretation by the Swiss-German scholar, Walther Hofer: "The war of 1939 . . . was long planned, exactly prepared for, and finally deliberately launched by the leader of the Third Reich, in sole responsibility so to speak, to be sure with the diplomatic support of the Soviet Government."[5]

This emphasis on Hitler's responsibility also appears in the eighth reading. It is taken from a brief history of Nazi Germany by two German scholars at the scholarly *Institut für Zeitgeschichte* (Institute for Contemporary History) in Munich. Hermann Mau and Helmut Krausnick present facts and unhesitatingly draw conclusions about Hitler's central responsibility for the war. In the ninth reading, writing in a terse "you-are-there" present-tense style, Maurice Baumont discusses the de-

[5] *Die Entfesselung des Zweiten Weltkrieges: Eine Studie über die internationalen Beziehungen im Sommer 1939* (Stuttgart, 2nd ed., 1955), 11.

scent into war as seen by a noted French historian. In the opinion of all of these authors of selections seven through nine, Hitler's determination to win *Lebensraum* ("living space" — additional territory), his snatch at Prague in March, 1939, and his willingness to risk a major war to secure gains from Poland led directly to the outbreak of hostilities on September 1, 1939. The war was essentially "Hitler's war," a result of both Hitler's design *and* Hitler's blunders. A detailed statement of this viewpoint was presented in the United States in 1960 in a popular book by William L. Shirer, *The Rise and Fall of the Third Reich.*

Then the publication in 1961 of a new book by a noted British historian, A. J. P. Taylor, caused an explosion of intellectual and political controversy; for Taylor argued that Hitler's 1939 aims were modest and that he had not planned war. The war, in Taylor's interpretation, came as a result not of design but of blunder, and mostly British blunder at that.

A more extreme interpretation was developed late in 1961 by an American writer, David L. Hoggan, who published in German a book entitled *The Forced War: Causes and Authors of the Second World War.* Hoggan's interpretation was closer to that of Charles C. Tansill than to Taylor's; in his bibliography Hoggan described the Tansill book as a "brilliant analysis," while his book presented Taylor as a British "court historian." Hoggan's thesis went far beyond Taylor's, but was like Taylor's in that it put responsibility on Great Britain. It argued that British foreign policy in 1938–1939 *deliberately sought,* finally with success, "to involve Germany in a new World War." It accused Britain of "aggression against Germany in the years 1914 and 1939" and contended that the Second World War came because of British plans "to destroy Germany," using Poland as a British tool. It was the British who gave the "blank check" of 1939 by guaranteeing their support of Poland. Because of the great threat of Communist Russia to all of Europe, the British and the Poles should have allowed Hitler to continue to broaden Germany's territorial holdings and sphere of influence. Instead, "Halifax's war policy, which had the secret blessings of Roosevelt and Stalin," frustrated last-minute efforts for a peaceful solution of the German-Polish problem. Hitler set his forces in motion on September 1, 1939, only when he was "left with no other choice," "only after he had reached the decision that war with Poland was in any case unavoidable."

Many observers thought it bitterly ironical that Tansill, Taylor, and Hoggan — British and American writers whose works were severely criticised by fellow historians at home — should tell Germans that Hitler's Germany had not been guilty after all for beginning the Second World War.

Hoggan was an unknown historian, and few serious scholars in either Germany or the United States were likely to pay much attention to his extreme views. Taylor, on the other hand, wrote at the peak of a career that had brought him international reputation. His arguments must be given serious consideration, even if you decide in the end that they are not convincing. If Taylor's (or even Hoggan's) interpretation is sound, it should be accepted by students of history, regardless of its political consequences; for the historian's enduring commitment must be to truth. It is important, therefore, to study the lengthy extracts from the Taylor volume — the tenth reading in this booklet — with special care. Is Taylor's writing persuasive? More important, is his evidence convincing? What evidence, if any, has he left out?

It is worth asking why Taylor published a book that on the surface at least seems to be favorable to Germany and even to Hitler. For in numerous previous books touching on German history, Taylor had revealed a strong antipathy to Germany.

How, then, can one explain the position Taylor took in his book of 1961 on the origins of World War II? Was Taylor simply striving for novel effect by swimming against the stream of historical interpretation? Perhaps so, since in most of his writings he has taken unorthodox positions on questions of interpretation. Was he pro-German, as it might appear at first thought? If so, this was certainly a new position, suddenly arrived at. Was he pro-Hitler? In absolving Hitler of sole responsibility, was he really trying to put the blame squarely upon the German people as a whole? Was he angry at Prime Minister Chamberlain because he did not give in to Hitler's demands in 1939 or because he failed to conclude a pact with the U.S.S.R.? In giving what appears to be a defense of appeasement, was Taylor really trying to popularize the idea of appeasing the U.S.S.R. in the 1960's?

This last possibility is suggested in the eleventh reading in this book, a review of the Taylor book by another noted British historian, Hugh R. Trevor-Roper. Above all, Trevor-Roper is concerned about a question of greater relevance to the student of history: Is Taylor's view of history a valid one? Is it arrived at through proper scholarly methodology? Seldom has one historian so devastatingly criticised the book of a colleague. Is Trevor-Roper's criticism of Taylor justified? Which author's view seems to be best supported by the factual evidence that you can glean from their readings, from others in this book, and from further study?

Historians seldom have literally the "last word" from a major historical personality about the central event in his life; Hitler gave his a few hours before he committed suicide on April 30, 1945. In his "Political Testament" of early April 29, the Führer wrote: "It is untrue that I or anybody else in Germany wanted war in 1939. It was wanted and provoked exclusively by those international statesmen who either were of Jewish origin or worked for Jewish interests." Against this self-defensive suicide note of 1945, the student of history must weigh Hitler's last written words, contained in a message of April 30 to Field Marshal Wilhelm Keitel: "The efforts and sacrifices of the German people in this war have been so great that I cannot believe that they have been in vain. The aim must still be to win territory in the East for the German people."

In evaluating these last records of Hitler's thoughts, one must consider his earlier writings; they are probably more reliable reflections of his ambitions and motives of 1939 than the clearly contradictory "last words" of 1945. Did Hitler plan to have a war? Was war inherent in his outlook on history and politics? Many historians since 1945 have been content to cite passages from Hitler's book of 1924, *Mein Kampf* (*My Struggle*), as proof that the would-be dictator even before 1933 had ambitious designs for conquest. Taylor dismissed this evidence as mere daydreaming on Hitler's part. But by coincidence, just as Taylor's book was being published, new evidence became available about Hitler's private views on foreign policy. In 1928 the ill-faring Führer of an unsuccessful party wrote a book that he never published. The manuscript was captured in 1945 by Allied armies and kept in custody for many years with millions of other German documents in a government depository near Washington. In 1961 the *Institut für Zeitgeschichte* (Institute for Contemporary History) published this hitherto secret Hitler manuscript, edited by two respected historians — one American, the other German. An American edition was published early in 1962, and extracts from it form the last reading in this book. Read this selection carefully. Should the foreign policy objectives Hitler outlined in 1928 be regarded as mere "daydreams," as "ambitions," or as "plans"? Do the ideas Hitler set forth in 1928 tend to confirm the views of Taylor or those of Trevor-Roper and other historians of six nations as set forth in this book?

When you have studied the readings in this book you will wish to consider their relevance to the present. If you conclude that appeasement of Germany encouraged war in 1939, what view of appeasement are you to take in the 1960's? If you conclude that the Nazi demands of 1938–1939 were legitimate at that time, would you consider German demands legitimate today? If you conclude that Germany's leaders must carry the chief responsibility for war in 1939, does that mean that the foreign policy of your nation should be hostile toward the Germany of the present? The Nazi leaders, the Poles, the British, and the French all decided that peace in 1939 could not be bought by backing down on their demands. Are there issues today on which the major powers should not be expected to back down, even at the risk of war? If you decide that war came in 1939 as a result of blunder, what does that tell you about your own responsibilities as a citizen in a democracy today?

Certainly one of those responsibilities is to consider the history, principles, possibilities, and limits of diplomacy. Even when diplomatic relations between nation states were emerging in the fifteenth century, diplomats disagreed about the function of diplomacy. Writing in 1436, Bernard du Rosier thought it the duty of diplomats "to confirm friendships . . . to make peace . . . to arrange past disputes, and remove the cause for future unpleasantness." About 1490 Ermolao Barbaro took a different view: "The first duty of an ambassador is . . . to do, say, advise and think whatever may best serve the preservation and aggrandizement of his own state." Both of these Renaissance philosophies were reflected in the conduct of diplomacy in 1939. The role of German diplomats was further complicated by the attitude of Nazi leaders toward them: "There is no doubt," Goebbels confided to his diary, "that a government is very wise not to inform its diplomats about changes in its policy." The corollary to this dictum was that Hitler frequently ignored the advice of Germany's professional diplomats. All of the men ultimately responsible for policy in 1939 — Hitler, Stalin, Beck, Mussolini, Daladier, Chamberlain, and Roosevelt — faced the eternal problem in diplomacy of making decisions on the basis of incomplete information about the policies of rival and friendly governments. Room is always left in diplomacy for imagination. For in the final analysis, writes Jacques de Bourbon-Busset (a French diplomat of the Cold War era), the decision is "always a choice between various opportunities, each of which is heavily loaded with inconveniences and even dangers." In the conduct of diplomacy as in the interpretation of history it is seldom possible to be absolutely certain that one's answers to important questions are the correct ones. It is easy to arrive at wrong answers in both if one ignores evidence — as Hitler in 1939 ignored the cautions given by his ambassadors in London, Washington, and elsewhere.

You are confronted in this book with divergent viewpoints, and this is as it should be. True learning in depth is accomplished in no other way. But the result should not be total confusion, nor a cynical assumption that in the study of history one interpretation is as valid as another. Your task in studying this book is to decide tentatively which two or three authors have most helped you approach what every student of history should try to approach, absolute truth about the "whats" and the "whys" of the past. As you read this book, note the pivotal events and their dates. Consider the interpretations of these events offered by each author. Then put all of the interpretations to a methodological test historians must use: decide to what extent each author's view is supported by empirical evidence, by the facts he presents and the facts that you can establish from all the readings. Ideally, you should not stop with this. Find out as much as you can about the professional qualifications and motives of each author, for these frequently have a bearing on the reliability of historians. And let this book be the beginning rather than the end of your study of the coming of the Second World War. Read full books and recent articles on the subject. Better still, go to the documents themselves. The "Suggestions for Additional Reading" at the end of this volume will be one pointer on your route.

Perhaps before your inquiry is over you will want to become an amateur or professional historian yourself. If this book stimulates your interest in history as a vocation or an avocation, it should end with a welcome: "There is still enough unexplored ground," it has been aptly said, "to keep the next generation of historians more than busy. . . ."[6]

6 Bernadotte E. Schmitt, quoted in *History as a Career: To Undergraduates Choosing a Profession* (Washington, 1961), 16; a brochure published by the American Historical Association.

[NOTE: Footnotes appeared in most of the original publications from which the following readings were taken. They are not reproduced here.]

IDENTIFICATIONS OF PERSONS
Mentioned in the Readings

AMERY, LEOPOLD S., *British Conservative, in House of Commons in 1939*

ASTAKHOV, GEORGI, *Counselor of the Soviet Embassy in Berlin in 1939*

ATTOLICO, BERNARDO, *Italian Ambassador in Berlin, 1939–1941*

BECK, COLONEL JÓZEF, *Polish Foreign Minister, 1932–1939*

BIDDLE, ANTHONY J. DREXEL, *United States Ambassador in Warsaw, 1937–1939*

BISMARCK, OTTO VON, *German Chancellor, 1871–1890*

BLOMBERG, GENERAL WERNER VON, *German Minister of War, 1933–1938*

BOEHM, *German admiral*

BONNET, GEORGES, *French Foreign Minister, 1938–1939*

BRÜNING, HEINRICH, *German Chancellor, 1930–1932*

BULLITT, WILLIAM C., *United States Ambassador in Moscow, 1933–1936; Ambassador in Paris, 1936–1940*

BURCKHARDT, CARL J., *Swiss scholar, League of Nations High Commissioner in Danzig, 1937–1939*

CARR, E. H., *British writer on international affairs*

CAVALLERO, UGO, *Italian general; Chief of the General Staff, 1940–1943*

CHAMBERLAIN, SIR NEVILLE, *British Prime Minister, 1937–1940*

CHURCHILL, WINSTON S., *in the 1930's British Conservative politician, critical of the policies of Chamberlain*

CIANO, COUNT GALEAZZO, *Mussolini's son-in-law and Italian Foreign Minister, 1936–1943*

CORBIN, CHARLES, *French Ambassador in London, 1933–1940*

COULONDRE, ROBERT, *French Ambassador in Moscow, 1938–1939*

DAHLERUS, BIRGER, *Swedish engineer and industrialist who performed liaison services for Goering in London, 1939*

DALADIER, ÉDOUARD, *French Premier, 1938–1940*

DILLON, CLARENCE, *American financier*

DIRKSEN, HERBERT VON, *German Ambassador in London in 1939*

DOUMENC, JOSEPH, *French general, leader of French military mission to Moscow in 1939*

ENSOR, SIR ROBERT, *British historian*

FORRESTAL, JAMES V., *Secretary of the Navy in the United States and first Secretary of Defense, 1947–1949*

FORSTER, ALBERT, *Nazi leader (Gauleiter) in Danzig in the 1930's*

FRANÇOIS-PONCET, ANDRÉ, *French Ambassador in Berlin, 1931–1938; in Rome, 1938–1940*

FRITSCH, WERNER VON, *Commander in Chief of the German Army, 1934–1938*

GIBBON, EDWARD, *English eighteenth-century historian*

GOEBBELS, PAUL JOSEF, *Reich Minister of Propaganda under Hitler*

GOERING, HERMANN, *Commander in Chief of the Luftwaffe (Air Force) in Nazi Germany and Head of the Office of the Four-Year Plan*

GREENWOOD, ARTHUR, *British ~~Conservative~~ Labour spokesman in House of Commons in 1939*

GRZYBOWSKI, M., *Polish Ambassador in Moscow, 1936–1939*

HÁCHA, EMIL, *President of Czechoslovakia, 1938–1939*

HAFFNER, SEBASTIAN, *British journalist*

HALIFAX, LORD EDWARD F.L.W., *British Foreign Secretary, 1938–1940*

HENDERSON, SIR NEVILE, *British Ambassador in Berlin, 1937–1939*

HINDENBURG, PAUL VON, *General and President of Germany, 1925–1934*

HITLER, ADOLF, *Chancellor of Germany and* Führer *(Leader), 1933–1945; Supreme Commander of the Armed Forces*

HOSSBACH, COLONEL (later General) FRIEDRICH, *Hitler's adjutant for the* Wehrmacht *(national defense services)*

HUDSON, ROBERT S., *Parliamentary Secretary to the British Department of Overseas Trade in 1939*

HULL, CORDELL, *Secretary of State of the United States, 1933–1944*

IRONSIDE, LORD EDMUND W., *British field marshal, Chief of Imperial General Staff, 1939–1940*

JODL, MAJOR GENERAL ALFRED, *Chief of the Operations Staff of the* Wehrmacht *High Command, August 23, 1939–1945*

KEITEL, FIELD MARSHAL WILHELM, *Chief of the High Command of the Armed Forces under Hitler, 1938–1945*

KENNEDY, JOSEPH P., *United States Ambassador in London, 1937–1940*

KHRUSHCHEV, NIKITA, *post-Stalin head of the U.S.S.R.*

KRESTINSKY, NIKOLAI, *Soviet Deputy-Commissar for Foreign Affairs under Maxim Litvinov*

LENIN, N., *founder of the Soviet regime in Russia*

LEOPOLD III, *King of the Belgians, 1934–1951*

LIPSKI, JÓZEF, *Polish Ambassador in Berlin, 1933–1939*

LITVINOV, MAXIM, *Soviet Commissar for Foreign Affairs, 1930–1939, favoring friendship with the western democracies*

LLOYD GEORGE, DAVID, *British Prime Minister in World War I; later Liberal member of the House of Commons*

LOTHIAN, LORD PHILIP HENRY, *British Ambassador in Washington, 1939–1940*

LUBOMIRSKI, PRINCE STEFAN, *Counselor of Polish Embassy in Berlin in 1939*

LUKASIEWICZ, JULES, *Polish Ambassador in Paris in 1939*

MACAULAY, THOMAS BABINGTON, *English nineteenth-century historian*

MACDONALD, RAMSAY, *leader of Labour Party and British Prime Minister, 1924, 1929–1935*

MAISKY, IVAN M., *Soviet Ambassador in London in 1939*

MARSHALL, VERNE, *Iowa newspaperman*

MIKOYAN, ANASTAS, *a leading Soviet Communist under Stalin and Khrushchev*

MOLOTOV, VYACHESLAV, *Soviet Commissar (after 1947, Minister) for Foreign Affairs, 1939–1956*

MOLTKE, HANS ADOLF VON, *German Ambassador in Warsaw in 1939*

MOŚCICKI, IGNACY, *President of Poland in 1939*

MUSSOLINI, BENITO, *Italian Premier, 1922–1943, and Head (Il Duce) of the Fascist Party*

NAGGIAR, PAUL-EMILE, *French Ambassador in Moscow in 1939*

NEURATH, KONSTANTIN VON, *German Foreign Minister, 1932–1938*

NOËL, LÉON, *French Ambassador in Warsaw, 1935–1939*

OGILVIE-FORBES, SIR GEORGE, *Counselor of the British Embassy in Berlin in 1939*

OSHIMA, GENERAL HIROSHI, *Japanese Ambassador in Berlin in 1939*

PAPEN, FRANZ VON, *German Chancellor, 1932; Ambassador to Austria, 1934–1938; Ambassador to Turkey, 1939–1944*

PAYART, M., *Counselor of French Embassy in Moscow in 1939*

PILSUDSKI, MARSHAL JÓZEF, *Polish dictator, 1920–1921, and 1926–1935*

PLUNKETT-ERNLE-ERLE-DRAX, ADMIRAL SIR REGINALD AYLMER, *head of British military mission in Moscow in 1939*

POTOCKI, COUNT JERZY, *Polish Ambassador in Washington, 1936–1941*

RAEDER, GRAND ADMIRAL ERICH, *Commander in Chief of the German Navy, 1935–1943*

REYNAUD, PAUL, *French Minister of Finance, 1938–1940; Premier, 1940*

RIBBENTROP, JOACHIM VON, *German Foreign Minister, 1938–1945*

RICHELIEU, CARDINAL, *seventeenth-century French statesman*

ROOSEVELT, FRANKLIN DELANO, *President of the United States, 1933–1945*

RYDZ-SMIGLY, MARSHAL EDOUARD, *Inspector General of the Polish Army in 1939*

SCHACHT, HJALMAR, *German Minister of Economics, 1934–1937; President of the Reichsbank, 1933–1939*

SCHMUNDT, COLONEL RUDOLF, *Hitler's adjutant for* Wehrmacht *affairs*

SCHNURRE, JULIUS, *Head of Economic Policy Division for Eastern Europe in the German Foreign Ministry in 1939*

SCHULENBURG, WERNER VON, *German Ambassador in Moscow, 1938–1941*

SCHUSCHNIGG, KURT VON, *Austrian Chancellor, 1934–1938*

SEEDS, SIR WILLIAM, *British Ambassador in Moscow in 1939*

SHIRATORI, TOSHIO, *Japanese Ambassador in Rome in 1939*

SIMON, SIR JOHN, *British Foreign Secretary, 1931–1935; Home Secretary, 1935–1937; Chancellor of the Exchequer, 1937–1940*

SMIGLY-RYDZ, *see Rydz-Smigly*

STALIN, JOSEF V., *head of the U.S.S.R., 1926–1953*

STRANG, SIR WILLIAM, *Head of the Central Department of the British Foreign Office and British representative in diplomatic negotiations in Moscow, 1939*

STRESEMANN, GUSTAV, *German Foreign Minister, 1923–1929*

TISO, JOZEF, *pro-German Minister-President of Slovakia in 1939*

TOSCANO, MARIO, *Italian historian*

VOROSHILOV, KLIMENTY E., *Soviet Commissar for Defense, 1925–1940*

WEIZSÄCKER, ERNST VON, *State Secretary in the German Foreign Office, 1938–1943*

WELCZECK, JOHANNES VON, *German Ambassador in Paris, 1936–1939*

WILHELMINA, *Queen of the Netherlands, 1890–1948*

WILSON, SIR HORACE, *confidential advisor to Prime Minister Neville Chamberlain and Permanent Secretary of the British Treasury in 1939*

WOHLTAT, HELMUTH, *an official of Hermann Goering's economic staff*

ZHDANOV, ANDREI A., *member of the Politburo (leading committee of the Communist Party of the Soviet Union) and in 1939 president of the Foreign Affairs Committee of the U.S.S.R.*

The Conflict of Opinion

"In the opinion of the Tribunal, the events of the days immediately preceding the 1st September 1939, demonstrate the determination of Hitler and his associates to carry out the declared intention of invading Poland at all costs, despite appeals from every quarter. . . . The Tribunal is fully satisfied by the evidence that the war initiated by Germany against Poland on the 1st September 1939, was most plainly an aggressive war. . . ."

— JUDGMENT OF THE INTERNATIONAL MILITARY
TRIBUNAL AT NUREMBERG, 1946

"All in all, the Soviet policy in this latter phase was one of shameless deception."

— WILLIAM L. LANGER and S. EVERETT GLEASON, 1952

"Whereas the USSR insisted on an agreement for combating aggression, Britain and France systematically rejected it, preferring to pursue a policy of isolating the USSR, a policy of . . . directing aggression to the East, against the USSR.

"The United States of America, far from counteracting that ruinous policy, backed it in every way."

— *Falsificators of History*, issued by the SOVIET INFORMATION BUREAU, 1948

"Nowadays it seems evident that the real Mad Hatter was Franklin D. Roosevelt, who pressed Chamberlain to give promises to the Poles when there was no possibility of fulfilling them. . . . Germany had been baited into a war with Britain and France when she would have preferred a conflict with Russia over the Ukraine."

— CHARLES CALLAN TANSILL, 1952

"[Polish Foreign Minister Józef] Beck's diplomatic career ended in complete disaster. . . . In one regard, however, Beck definitely deserves respect. When the final test came, he did not yield. In a desperate situation, partly of his own making, he took an unprovocative but courageous stand."

— HENRY L. ROBERTS, 1953

"The [German-Italian] Pact of Steel was a symptom rather than a factor in the history of 1939. . . ."

— L. B. NAMIER, 1950

"Over and over, through the spring and summer of 1939 the British and French Governments had said they would fight if Germany attacked Poland. These warnings went unheeded. . . . Now Hitler was confronted by the despised Poles. . . . In a last desperate effort to break the will of his opponents, he promised the hated Communists more for neutrality than he could win from war against Poland."

— RAYMOND J. SONTAG, 1957

"In the early hours of September 1st . . . Germany attacked Poland. Hitler had ordered the attack knowing that he was risking a world war. . . ."

— HERMANN MAU and HELMUT KRAUSNICK, 1953, 1956, 1961

"By . . . the end of August, Hitler has lost his illusions: he no longer counts on the abstention of Great Britain and France. On the contrary, he believes in what he calls 'the great struggle.' . . . The Führer is in a hurry to start the campaign. . . ."

— MAURICE BAUMONT, 1951

"In principle and doctrine, Hitler was no more wicked and unscrupulous than many other contemporary statesmen. . . . Danzig was the most justified of German grievances. . . . The war of 1939, far from being premeditated, was a mistake, the result on both sides of diplomatic blunders."

— A. J. P. TAYLOR, 1961

"If Mr. Taylor's cardinal assumptions about Hitler's character and purpose are, to say the least, questionable, what are we to say of his use of evidence to illustrate them? . . . This casuistical defence of Hitler's foreign policy will not only do harm by supporting neo-Nazi mythology: it will also do harm, perhaps irreparable harm, to Mr. Taylor's reputation as a serious historian."

— HUGH R. TREVOR-ROPER, 1961

"The National Socialist movement . . . will always let its foreign policy be determined by the necessity to secure the space necessary to the life of our people. . . . This territory can be only in the East . . ."

— ADOLF HITLER, 1928

VICTORY'S VERDICT: BLUNDER THROWN OUT OF COURT

THE NUREMBERG JUDGMENT

The Nuremberg trial of political and military leaders of Nazi Germany and leading organizations of the Nazi state lasted from November 20, 1945, to October 1, 1946, when the four-power Tribunal rendered its judgment. Defendants were tried on four charges: crimes against peace "by planning, preparation, initiation, and waging of wars of aggression"; war crimes; crimes against humanity; and participation in "a common plan or conspiracy to commit all these crimes." Twelve Nazi leaders were sentenced to death and several others to imprisonment, after some were found guilty on all four counts and others on some of them. The International Military Tribunal heard dozens of witnesses for and against the defendants, and received depositions from thousands of others. As the Tribunal itself reported, "Much of the evidence . . . on behalf of the prosecution was documentary evidence. . . . The case, therefore, against the defendants rests in a large measure on documents of their own making, the authenticity of which has not been challenged except in one or two cases." The judgment of October 1, 1946, from which this reading is taken, was signed by all eight members and alternate members of the Tribunal, including Major General I. T. Nikitchenko and Lt. Col. A. F. Volchkov, member and alternate member of the Tribunal for the U.S.S.R.

URING the years immediately following Hitler's appointment as Chancellor, the Nazi Government set about reorganizing the economic life of Germany, and in particular the armament industry. This was done on a vast scale and with extreme thoroughness.

It was necessary to lay a secure financial foundation for the building of armaments, and in April 1936, the defendant Goering was appointed coordinator for raw materials and foreign exchange, and empowered to supervise all state and party activities in these fields. In this capacity he brought together the War Minister, the Minister of Economics, the Reich Finance Minister, the President of the Reichsbank, and the Prussian Finance Minister to discuss problems connected with war mobilization, and on the 27th May 1936, in addressing these men, Goering opposed any financial limitation of war production and added that "all measures are to be considered from the standpoint of an assured waging of war." At the Party Rally in Nurnberg in 1936, Hitler announced the establishment of the Four-Year Plan and the appointment of Goering as the Plenipotentiary in charge. Goering was already engaged in building a strong air force and on the 8th July 1938, he announced to a number of leading German aircraft manufacturers that the German Air Force was already superior in quality and quantity to the English. On the 14th October 1938, at another conference, Goering announced that Hitler had

From *Nazi Conspiracy and Aggression: Opinion and Judgment,* published by the Office of United States Chief of Counsel for Prosecution of Axis Criminality (Washington, 1947), pp. 12–13, 16–21, 27–34.

instructed him to organize a gigantic armament program, which would make insignificant all previous achievements. He said that he had been ordered to build as rapidly as possible an air force five times as large as originally planned, to increase the speed of the rearmament of the navy and army, and to concentrate on offensive weapons, principally heavy artillery and heavy tanks. He then laid down a specific program designed to accomplish these ends. The extent to which rearmament had been accomplished was stated by Hitler in his memorandum of 9 October 1939, after the campaign in Poland. He said:

The military application of our people's strength has been carried through to such an extent that within a short time at any rate it cannot be markedly improved upon by any manner of effort.

The warlike equipment of the German people is at present larger in quantity and better in quality for a greater number of German divisions than in the year 1914. The weapons themselves, taking a substantial cross-section, are more modern than is the case of any other country in the world at this time. They have just proved their supreme war worthiness in their victorious campaign . . . There is no evidence available to show that any country in the world disposes of a better total ammunition stock than the Reich . . . The A. A. artillery is not equalled by any country in the world.

In this reorganization of the economic life of Germany for military purposes, the Nazi Government found the German armament industry quite willing to cooperate, and to play its part in the rearmament program. . . .

The first acts of aggression referred to in the indictment are the seizure of Austria and Czechoslovakia; and the first war of aggression charged in the indictment is the war against Poland begun on the 1st September 1939.

Before examining that charge it is necessary to look more closely at some of the events which preceded these acts of aggression. The war against Poland did not come suddenly out of an otherwise clear sky; the evidence has made it plain that this war of aggression, as well as the seizure of Austria and Czechoslovakia, was premeditated and carefully prepared, and was not undertaken until the moment was thought opportune for it to be carried through as a definite part of the preordained scheme and plan.

For the aggressive designs of the Nazi Government were not accidents arising out of the immediate political situation in Europe and the world; they were a deliberate and essential part of Nazi foreign policy.

From the beginning, the National Socialist movement claimed that its object was to unite the German people in the consciousness of their mission and destiny, based on inherent qualities of race, and under the guidance of the Fuehrer.

For its achievement, two things were deemed to be essential: The disruption of the European order as it had existed since the Treaty of Versailles, and the creation of a Greater Germany beyond the frontiers of 1914. This necessarily involved the seizure of foreign territories.

War was seen to be inevitable, or at the very least, highly probable, if these purposes were to be accomplished. The German people, therefore, with all their resources, were to be organized as a great political-military army, schooled to obey without question any policy decreed by the State.

In "Mein Kampf" Hitler had made this view quite plain. It must be remembered that "Mein Kampf" was no mere private diary in which the secret thoughts of Hitler were set down. Its contents were rather proclaimed from the house tops. It was used in the schools and universities and among the Hitler Youth, in the SS and the SA, and among the German people generally, even down to the presentation of an official copy to all newly married people. By the year 1945 over 6½ million copies had been circulated. The general contents are well known. Over and over again

Hitler asserted his belief in the necessity of force as the means of solving international problems, as in the following quotation:

The soil on which we now live was not a gift bestowed by Heaven on our forefathers. They had to conquer it by risking their lives. So also in the future, our people will not obtain territory, and therewith the means of existence, as a favor from any other people, but will have to win it by the power of a triumphant sword.

"Mein Kampf" contains many such passages, and the extolling of force as an instrument of foreign policy is openly proclaimed.

The precise objectives of this policy of force are also set forth in detail. The very first page of the book asserts that "German-Austria must be restored to the great German Motherland," not on economic grounds, but because "people of the same blood should be in the same Reich."

The restoration of the German frontiers of 1914 is declared to be wholly insufficient, and if Germany is to exist at all, it must be as a world power with the necessary territorial magnitude.

"Mein Kampf" is quite explicit in stating where the increased territory is to be found:

Therefore we National Socialists have purposely drawn a line through the line of conduct followed by prewar Germany in foreign policy. We put an end to the perpetual Germanic march towards the south and west of Europe, and turn our eyes towards the lands of the east. We finally put a stop to the colonial and trade policy of the prewar times, and pass over to the territorial policy of the future.

But when we speak of new territory in Europe today, we must think principally of Russia and the border states subject to her.

"Mein Kampf" is not to be regarded as a mere literary exercise, nor as an inflexible policy or plan incapable of modification.

Its importance lies in the unmistakable attitude of aggression revealed throughout its pages.

Evidence from captured documents has revealed that Hitler held four secret meetings to which the Tribunal proposes to make special reference because of the light they shed upon the question of the common plan and aggressive war.

These meetings took place on the 5th November 1937, the 23d of May 1939, the 22d of August 1939, and the 23d of November 1939.

At these meetings important declarations were made by Hitler as to his purposes, which are quite unmistakable in their terms.

The documents which record what took place at these meetings have been subject to some criticism at the hands of defending counsel.

Their essential authenticity is not denied, but it is said, for example, that they do not propose to be verbatim transcripts of the speeches they record, that the document dealing with the meeting on the 5th November 1937, was dated 5 days after the meeting had taken place, and that the two documents dealing with the meeting of August 22, 1939 differ from one another, and are unsigned.

Making the fullest allowance for criticism of this kind, the Tribunal is of the opinion that the documents are documents of the highest value, and that their authenticity and substantial truth are established.

They are obviously careful records of the events they describe, and they have been preserved as such in the archives of the German Government, from whose custody they were captured. Such documents could never be dismissed as inventions, nor even as inaccurate or distorted; they plainly record events which actually took place.

It will perhaps be useful to deal first of all with the meeting of the 23d November 1939, when Hitler called his supreme commanders together. A record was made of what was said, by one of those present.

At the date of the meeting, Austria and Czechoslovakia had been incorporated into the German Reich, Poland had been conquered by the German armies, and the war with Great Britain and France was still in its static phase. The moment was opportune for a review of past events. Hitler informed the commanders that the purpose of the conference was to give them an idea of the world of his thoughts, and to tell them his decision. He thereupon reviewed his political task since 1919, and referred to the secession of Germany from the League of Nations, the denunciation of the Disarmament Conference, the order for rearmament, the introduction of compulsory armed service, the occupation of the Rhineland, the seizure of Austria, and the action against Czechoslovakia. He stated:

One year later, Austria came; this step also was considered doubtful. It brought about a considerable reinforcement of the Reich. The next step was Bohemia, Moravia, and Poland. This step also was not possible to accomplish in one campaign. First of all, the western fortification had to be finished. It was not possible to reach the goal in one effort. It was clear to me from the first moment that I could not be satisfied with the Sudeten German territory. That was only a partial solution. The decision to march into Bohemia was made. Then followed the erection of the Protectorate and with that the basis for the action against Poland was laid, but I wasn't quite clear at that time whether I should start first against the east and then in the west or vice versa . . . Basically I did not organize the armed forces in order not to strike. The decision to strike was always in me. Earlier or later I wanted to solve the problem. Under pressure it was decided that the east was to be attacked first.

This address, reviewing past events and reaffirming the aggressive intentions present from the beginning, puts beyond any question of doubt the character of the actions against Austria and Czechoslovakia, and the war against Poland.

For they had all been accomplished according to plan; and the nature of that plan must now be examined in a little more detail.

At the meeting of the 23d November 1939, Hitler was looking back to things accomplished; at the earlier meetings now to be considered, he was looking forward, and revealing his plans to his confederates. The comparison is instructive.

The meeting held at the Reich Chancellery in Berlin on the 5th November 1937 was attended by Lieutenant Colonel Hossbach, Hitler's personal adjutant, who compiled a long note of the proceedings, which he dated the 10th November 1937 and signed.

The persons present were Hitler, and the defendants Goering, von Neurath, and Raeder, in their capacities as Commander in Chief of the Luftwaffe, Reich Foreign Minister, and Commander in Chief of the Navy respectively, General von Blomberg, Minister of War, and General von Fritsch, the Commander in Chief of the Army.

Hitler began by saying that the subject of the conference was of such high importance that in other States it would have taken place before the Cabinet. He went on to say that the subject matter of his speech was the result of his detailed deliberations, and of his experiences during his 4½ years of government. He requested that the statements he was about to make should be looked upon in the case of his death as his last will and testament. Hitler's main theme was the problem of living space, and he discussed various possible solutions, only to set them aside. He then said that the seizure of living space on the continent of Europe was therefore necessary, expressing himself in these words:

It is not a case of conquering people but of conquering agriculturally useful space. It would also be more to the purpose to seek raw material producing territory in Europe directly adjoining the Reich and not overseas, and this solution would have to be brought into effect for one or two generations . . . The history of all times — Roman Empire, British Empire — has proved that every space expansion can only be effected by breaking resistance and taking risks. Even set-backs are unavoidable; neither formerly nor today has space been found without an owner; the attacker always comes up against the proprietor.

He concluded with this observation:

The question for Germany is where the greatest possible conquest could be made at the lowest cost.

Nothing could indicate more plainly the aggressive intentions of Hitler, and the events which soon followed showed the reality of his purpose. It is impossible to accept the contention that Hitler did not actually mean war; for after pointing out that Germany might expect the opposition of England and France, and analyzing the strength and the weakness of those powers in particular situations, he continued:

The German question can be solved only by way of force, and this is never without risk . . . If we place the decision to apply force with risk at the head of the following expositions, then we are left to reply to the questions "when" and "how." In this regard we have to decide upon three different cases.

The first of these three cases set forth a hypothetical international situation, in which he would take action not later than 1943 to 1945, saying:

If the Fuehrer is still living then it will be his irrevocable decision to solve the German space problem not later than 1943 to 1945. The necessity for action before 1943 to 1945 will come under consideration in cases 2 and 3.

The second and third cases to which Hitler referred show the plain intention to seize Austria and Czechoslovakia, and in this connection Hitler said:

For the improvement of our military-political position, it must be our first aim in every case of entanglement by war to conquer Czechoslovakia and Austria simultaneously in order to remove any threat from the flanks in case of a possible advance westwards.

He further added:

The annexation of the two States to Germany militarily and politically would constitute a considerable relief, owing to shorter and better frontiers, the freeing of fighting personnel for other purposes, and the possibility of reconstituting new armies up to a strength of about twelve divisions.

This decision to seize Austria and Czechoslovakia was discussed in some detail; the action was to be taken as soon as a favorable opportunity presented itself.

The military strength which Germany had been building up since 1933 was now to be directed at the two specific countries, Austria and Czechoslovakia.

The defendant Goering testified that he did not believe at that time that Hitler actually meant to attack Austria and Czechoslovakia, and that the purpose of the conference was only to put pressure on von Fritsch to speed up the rearmament of the Army.

The defendant Raeder testified that neither he, nor von Fritsch, nor von Blomberg, believed that Hitler actually meant war, a conviction which the defendant Raeder claims that he held up to the 22d August 1939. The basis of this conviction was his hope that Hitler would obtain a "political solution" of Germany's problems. But all that this means, when examined, is the belief that Germany's position would be so good, and Germany's armed might so overwhelming, that the territory desired could be obtained without fighting for it. It must be remembered too that Hitler's declared intention with regard to Austria was actually carried out within a little over 4 months from the date of the meeting, and within less than a year the first portion of Czechoslovakia was absorbed, and Bohemia and Moravia a few months later. If any doubts had existed in the minds of any of his hearers in November 1937, after March of 1939 there could no longer be any question that Hitler was in deadly earnest in his decision to resort to war. The Tribunal is satisfied that Lieutenant Colonel Hossbach's account of the meeting is substantially correct, and that those present knew that Austria and Czechoslovakia would be annexed by Germany at the first possible opportunity. . . .

By March 1939 the plan to annex Austria and Czechoslovakia, which had been discussed by Hitler at the meeting of the 5th November 1937, had been accomplished. The time had now come for the German leaders to consider further acts of aggression, made more possible of attainment because of that accomplishment.

On the 23d May 1939, a meeting was held in Hitler's study in the new Reich Chancellery in Berlin. Hitler announced his decision to attack Poland and gave his reasons, and discussed the effect the decision might have on other countries. In point of time, this was the second of the important meetings to which reference has already been made, and in order to appreciate the full significance of what was said and done, it is necessary to state shortly some of the main events in the history of German-Polish relations.

As long ago as the year 1925 an Arbitration Treaty between Germany and Poland had been made at Locarno, providing for the settlement of all disputes between the two countries. On the 26th January 1934, a German-Polish declaration of nonaggression was made, signed on behalf of the German Government by the defendant von Neurath.[1] On the 30th January 1934, and again on the 30th January 1937, Hitler made speeches in the Reichstag in which he expressed his view that Poland and Germany could work together in harmony and peace. On the 20th February 1938, Hitler made a third speech in the Reichstag in the course of which he said with regard to Poland:

And so the way to a friendly understanding

[1] Whenever in these readings you encounter names of persons whose positions are unknown to you, please refer to the "Identifications of Persons" in the front of this booklet. [Editor's Note]

has been successfully paved, an understanding which, beginning with Danzig, has today, in spite of the attempts of certain mischief makers, succeeded in finally taking the poison out of the relations between Germany and Poland and transforming them into a sincere, friendly cooperation. Relying on her friendships, Germany will not leave a stone unturned to save that ideal which provides the foundation for the task which is ahead of us — peace.

On the 26th September 1938, in the middle of the crisis over the Sudetenland, Hitler made the speech in Berlin which has already been quoted, and announced that he had informed the British Prime Minister that when the Czechoslovakian problem was solved there would be no more territorial problems for Germany in Europe. Nevertheless, on the 24th November of the same year, an OKW directive was issued to the German armed forces to make preparations for an attack upon Danzig; it stated:

The Fuehrer has ordered: (1) Preparations are also to be made to enable the Free State of Danzig to be occupied by German troops by surprise.

In spite of having ordered military preparations for the occupation of Danzig, Hitler, on the 30th January 1939, said in a speech in the Reichstag:

During the troubled months of the past year, the friendship between Germany and Poland has been one of the reassuring factors in the political life of Europe.

Five days previously, on the 25th January 1939, von Ribbentrop said in the course of a speech in Warsaw:

Thus Poland and Germany can look forward to the future with full confidence in the solid basis of their mutual relations.

Following the occupation of Bohemia and Moravia by Germany on the 15th March 1939, which was a flagrant breach of the Munich Agreement, Great Britain gave an assurance to Poland on the 31st March 1939, that in the event of any action which clearly threatened Polish independence, and which the Polish Government accordingly considered it vital to resist with their national forces, Great Britain would feel itself bound at once to lend Poland all the support in its power. The French Government took the same stand. It is interesting to note in this connection, that one of the arguments frequently presented by the defense in the present case is that the defendants were induced to think that their conduct was not in breach of international law by the acquiescence of other powers. The declarations of Great Britain and France showed, at least, that this view could be held no longer.

On the 3d April 1939, a revised OKW directive was issued to the armed forces, which after referring to the question of Danzig made reference to Fall Weiss (the military code name for the German invasion of Poland) and stated:

The Fuehrer has added the following directions to Fall Weiss: (1) Preparations must be made in such a way that the operation can be carried out at any time from the 1st September 1939 onwards. (2) The High Command of the Armed Forces has been directed to draw up a precise timetable for Fall Weiss and to arrange by conferences the synchronized timings between the three branches of the Armed Forces.

On the 11th of April 1939, a further directive was signed by Hitler and issued to the armed forces, and in one of the annexes to that document the words occur:

Quarrels with Poland should be avoided. Should Poland, however, adopt a threatening attitude toward Germany, "a final settlement" will be necessary, notwithstanding the pact with Poland. The aim is then to destroy Polish military strength, and to create in the east a situation which satisfies the requirements of defense. The Free State of Danzig will be incorporated into Germany at the outbreak of the conflict at the latest. Policy aims at limiting the war to Poland, and this is considered possible in view of the internal crisis in France, and British restraint as a result of this.

In spite of the contents of those two directives, Hitler made a speech in the Reichstag on the 28th of April 1939, in which, after describing the Polish Government's alleged rejection of an offer he had made with regard to Danzig and the Polish Corridor, he stated:

I have regretted greatly this incomprehensible attitude of the Polish Government, but that alone is not the decisive fact; the worst is that now Poland like Czechoslovakia a year ago believes, under the pressure of a lying international campaign, that it must call up its troops, although Germany on her part has not called up a single man, and had not thought of proceeding in any way against Poland. . . . The intention to attack on the part of Germany which was merely invented by the international Press . . .

It was 4 weeks after making this speech that Hitler, on the 23d May 1939, held the important military conference to which reference has already been made. Among the persons present were the defendants Goering, Raeder, and Keitel. The adjutant on duty that day was Lieutenant Colonel Schmundt, and he made a record of what happened, certifying it with his signature as a correct record.

The purpose of the meeting was to enable Hitler to inform the heads of the armed forces and their staffs of his views on the political situation and his future aims. After analyzing the political situation and reviewing the course of events since 1933, Hitler announced his decision to attack Poland. He admitted that the quarrel with Poland over Danzig was not the reason for this attack, but the necessity for Germany to enlarge her living space and secure her food supplies. He said:

The solution of the problem demands courage. The principle by which one evades solving the problem by adapting oneself to circumstances is inadmissible. Circumstances must rather be adapted to needs. This is impossible without invasion of foreign states or attacks upon foreign property.

Later in his address he added:

There is therefore no question of sparing Poland, and we are left with the decision to attack Poland at the first suitable opportunity. We cannot expect a repetition of the Czech affair. There will be war. Our task is to isolate Poland. The success of the isolation will be decisive. . . . The isolation of Poland is a matter of skillful politics.

Lieutenant Colonel Schmundt's record of the meeting reveals that Hitler fully realized the possibility of Great Britain and France coming to Poland's assistance. If, therefore, the isolation of Poland could not be achieved, Hitler was of the opinion that Germany should attack Great Britain and France first, or at any rate should concentrate primarily on the war in the West, in order to defeat Great Britain and France quickly, or at least to destroy their effectiveness. Nevertheless, Hitler stressed that war with England and France would be a life and death struggle, which might last a long time, and that preparations must be made accordingly.

During the weeks which followed this conference, other meetings were held and directives were issued in preparation for the war. The defendant von Ribbentrop was sent to Moscow to negotiate a non-aggression pact with the Soviet Union.

On the 22d August 1939 there took place the important meeting of that day, to which reference has already been made. The prosecution have put in evidence two unsigned captured documents which appear to be records made of this meeting by persons who were present. The first document is headed: "The Fuehrer's speech to the Commanders in Chief on the 22nd August 1939 . . ." The purpose of the speech was to announce the decision to make war on Poland at once, and Hitler began by saying:

It was clear to me that a conflict with Poland had to come sooner or later. I had already made this decision in the spring, but I thought that I would first turn against the West in a few years, and only afterwards against the East . . . I wanted to establish an acceptable relationship with Poland in order to fight first against the West. But this plan, which was agreeable to me, could not be executed since essential points have changed. It became clear to me that Poland would attack us in case of a conflict with the West.

Hitler then went on to explain why he had decided that the most favorable moment had arrived for starting the war. "Now," said Hitler, "Poland is in the position in which I wanted her . . . I am only afraid that at the last moment some Schweinhund will make a proposal for mediation . . . A beginning has been made for the destruction of England's hegemony."

This document closely resembles one of the documents put in evidence on behalf of the defendant Raeder. This latter document consists of a summary of the same speech, compiled on the day it was made, by one Admiral Boehm, from notes he had taken during the meeting. In substance it says that the moment had arrived to settle the dispute with Poland by military invasion, that although a conflict between Germany and the West was unavoidable in the long run, the likelihood of Great Britain and France coming to Poland's assistance was not great, and that even if a war in the West should come about, the first aim should be the crushing of the Polish military strength. It also contains a statement by Hitler that an appropriate propaganda reason for invading Poland would be given, the truth or falsehood of which was unimportant, since "the Right lies in Victory."

The second unsigned document put in evidence by the prosecution is headed: "Second Speech by the Fuehrer on the 22d August 1939," and it is in the form of notes of the main points made by Hitler. Some of these are as follows:

Everybody shall have to make a point of it

that we were determined from the beginning to fight the Western Powers. Struggle for life or death . . . destruction of Poland in the foreground. The aim is elimination of living forces, not the arrival at a certain line. Even if war should break out in the West, the destruction of Poland shall be the primary objective. I shall give a propagandist cause for starting the war — never mind whether it be plausible or not. The victor shall not be asked later on whether we told the truth or not. In starting and making a war, not the Right is what matters, but Victory . . The start will be ordered probably by Saturday morning. (That is to say, the 26th August.)

In spite of it being described as a second speech, there are sufficient points of similarity with the two previously mentioned documents to make it appear very probable that this is an account of the same speech, not as detailed as the other two, but in substance the same.

These three documents establish that the final decision as to the date of Poland's destruction, which had been agreed upon and planned earlier in the year, was reached by Hitler shortly before the 22d August 1939. They also show that although he hoped to be able to avoid having to fight Great Britain and France as well, he fully realized that there was a risk of this happening, but it was a risk which he was determined to take.

The events of the last days of August confirm this determination. On the 22d August 1939, the same day as the speech just referred to, the British Prime Minister wrote a letter to Hitler, in which he said:

Having thus made our position perfectly clear, I wish to repeat to you my conviction that war between our two peoples would be the greatest calamity that could occur.

On the 23d August, Hitler replied:

The question of the treatment of European problems on a peaceful basis is not a decision which rests with Germany, but primarily on those who since the crime committed by the Versailles Dictate have stubbornly and consistently opposed any peaceful revision. Only after a change of spirit on the part of the responsible Powers can there be any real change in the relationship between England and Germany.

There followed a number of appeals to Hitler to refrain from forcing the Polish issue to the point of war. These were from President Roosevelt on the 24th and 25th August; from His Holiness the Pope on the 24th and 31st August; and from M. Daladier, the Prime Minister of France, on the 26th August. All these appeals fell on deaf ears.

On the 25th August, Great Britain signed a pact of mutual assistance with Poland, which reinforced the understanding she had given to Poland earlier in the year. This coupled with the news of Mussolini's unwillingness to enter the war on Germany's side, made Hitler hesitate for a moment. The invasion of Poland, which was timed to start on the 26th August, was postponed until a further attempt had been made to persuade Great Britain not to intervene. Hitler offered to enter into a comprehensive agreement with Great Britain, once the Polish question had been settled. In reply to this, Great Britain made a countersuggestion for the settlement of the Polish dispute by negotiation. On the 29th August, Hitler informed the British Ambassador that the German Government, though skeptical as to the result, would be prepared to enter into direct negotiations with a Polish emissary, provided he arrived in Berlin with plenipotentiary powers by midnight of the following day, August 30. The Polish Government were informed of this, but with the example of Schuschnigg and Hácha before them, they decided not to send such an emissary. At midnight on the 30th August the defendant von Ribbentrop read to the British Ambassador at top speed a document containing the first precise formulation of the German demands against Poland. He refused, however, to give the Ambassador a copy of this, and stated that in any case it was too late now, since no Polish plenipotentiary had arrived.

In the opinion of the Tribunal, the manner in which these negotiations were conducted by Hitler and von Ribbentrop showed that they were not entered into in good faith or with any desire to maintain peace, but solely in the attempt to prevent Great Britain and France from honoring their obligations to Poland.

Parallel with these negotiations were the unsuccessful attempts made by Goering to effect the isolation of Poland by persuading Great Britain not to stand by her pledged word, through the services of one Birger Dahlerus, a Swede. Dahlerus, who was called as a witness by Goering, had a considerable knowledge of England and of things English, and in July 1939 was anxious to bring about a better understanding between England and Germany, in the hope of preventing a war between the two countries. He got into contact with Goering as well as with official circles in London, and during the latter part of August, Goering used him as an unofficial intermediary to try and deter the British Government from their opposition to Germany's intentions toward Poland. Dahlerus, of course, had no knowledge at the time of the decision which Hitler had secretly announced on the 22d August, nor of the German military directives for the attack on Poland which were already in existence. As he admitted in his evidence, it was not until the 26th September, after the conquest of Poland was virtually complete, that he first realized that Goering's aim all along had been to get Great Britain's consent to Germany's seizure of Poland.

After all attempts to persuade Germany to agree to a settlement of her dispute with Poland on a reasonable basis had failed, Hitler, on the 31st August, issued his final directive, in which he announced that the attack on Poland would start in the early morning of the 1st September, and gave instructions as to what action would be taken if Great Britain and France should enter the war in defense of Poland.

In the opinion of the Tribunal, the events of the days immediately preceding the 1st September 1939, demonstrate the determination of Hitler and his associates to carry out the declared intention of invading Poland at all costs, despite appeals from every quarter. With the ever increasing evidence before him that this intention would lead to war with Great Britain and France as well, Hitler was resolved not to depart from the course he had set for himself. The Tribunal is fully satisfied by the evidence that the war initiated by Germany against Poland on the 1st September 1939, was most plainly an aggressive war, which was to develop in due course into a war which embraced almost the whole world, and resulted in the commission of countless crimes, both against the laws and customs of war, and against humanity.

COLD WAR ERA REVISION: STALIN'S "BLANK CHECK" OF 1939

WILLIAM L. LANGER AND S. EVERETT GLEASON

The Nuremberg judgment blamed no nation but Nazi Germany for the outbreak of World War II. Western appeasement before 1939 was not on trial, nor was the U.S.S.R. rebuked for its obvious appeasement in the Nazi-Soviet Pact of August 23, 1939. The authors of the following reading criticized both, but found the U.S.S.R. largely responsible for the failure to stop Hitler by East-West diplomatic agreements in August, 1939. William L. Langer, distinguished Harvard historian, published several impressive studies of pre-1914 diplomacy before serving with the O.S.S. (Office of Strategic Services) in World War II. A specialist before the war in medieval history at Harvard and Amherst, S. Everett Gleason also served with the O.S.S. in the Second World War. The joint study from which the following reading is taken was the product of several years of research, sponsored by the Council on Foreign Relations in New York. This reading offers a detailed account of both the French-British-Soviet and the Nazi-Soviet negotiations of 1939. A successful outcome of the former might well have prevented Hitler from launching World War II; the conclusion of the latter virtually guaranteed that he would start it. If the outcome of these negotiations was primarily the fault of the Western powers, they bear a major responsibility for the outbreak of the war. If the outcome was the fault of the Soviet leaders, their responsibility for the war is second only to that of Hitler himself, and perhaps even greater than his; for Hitler viewed the Nazi-Soviet Pact as a "blank check" for his war against Poland. To get it, he betrayed his own anti-Communist principles and agreed to the first expansion of the U.S.S.R. since 1921, to the movement of Soviet forces westward into Central-Eastern Europe. In 1945 it would be impossible for Roosevelt and Churchill to deprive Stalin of what Hitler had given him in 1939.

ON May 3, 1939, the Kremlin announced that Maxim Litvinov, for many years Commissar for Foreign Affairs, had been relieved of his duties and that Vyacheslav Molotov would take over his position. Throughout the world this item of news created a sensation. It seemed obviously important, though utterly baffling. In diplomatic circles there was little inclination to accept Soviet statements that the change implied no shift in policy. Neither was it thought that Litvinov's reputed ill-health supplied an adequate explanation. What seemed most significant was that Litvinov was a Jew, that he was notoriously anti-German, and that for years he had been the vociferous champion of a system of collective security. The least that could be expected was that his dismissal presaged the abandonment of the policy or tactics theretofore supported by the Soviet leaders. The question of the hour was, then, what

11

form future Soviet policy was apt to take.
. . .

While Mr. Chamberlain stood his ground, the British public clamored for a pact with Moscow. On May 19, 1939, a rather acrimonious debate developed in Parliament, in the course of which Mr. Lloyd George warned against underestimating Soviet power and stressed the importance of a full-fledged alliance with Russia: "For months," he complained, "we having been staring this powerful gift horse in the mouth." Churchill, too, declared that "without an effective eastern front, there can be no satisfactory defence of our interests in the West, and without Russia there can be no effective eastern front." To which the Prime Minister replied that he simply could not help feeling "that there is a sort of veil, a sort of wall" between the British and the Soviet Governments, which he found it extremely difficult to penetrate. Under the circumstances he must walk warily. It was important not to divide Europe into two hostile blocs and it was equally important to consider the objections of other states. Though Mr. Churchill tried to brush aside these refinements and admonished the Government that if it cast aside the indispensable aid of Soviet Russia it would lead the country "in the worst of all ways into the worst of all wars," there was no sign that Mr. Chamberlain would yield to public pressure.

On May 20, 1939, Lord Halifax stopped at Paris on his way to the meeting of the Council of the League of Nations at Geneva. He had hoped to find Mr. Molotov at the meeting, but at the last minute the Kremlin had instructed Mr. Maisky, the Soviet Ambassador in London, to substitute. After conferences first with M. Bonnet and later with Mr. Maisky, the British Foreign Secretary convinced himself that an arrangement with Russia was essential and that it would probably have to be concluded on Soviet terms. On his return to London he secured support in the Cabinet and Mr. Chamberlain reluctantly agreed to accept the Soviet proposal in substance. To save face, however, the British decided to put the whole project under the League Covenant and to mask the phraseology. Their new proposal, dispatched on May 25, 1939, was that the three contracting powers, acting in accordance with the principles of the League, should lend each other immediate assistance (1) if any one of them became involved in war because of aid given a European country which they had guaranteed against aggression; (2) if any one of them became involved in war because of aid rendered a nonguaranteed country which, being the victim of aggression, defended itself and requested aid; (3) if any European power attacked one of the contracting parties while the latter was engaged in taking action in accord with Article XVI of the Covenant. The signatories were to consult whenever circumstances threatened to call for the implementation of these pledges.

The French Foreign Office, while recognizing the imperfections of this compromise, thought the new note covered the essential points and hoped for the conclusion of the pact within a week. But Molotov refused to reduce his demands by even one tittle. He objected to bringing in the League, but above all insisted that Soviet aid to the Baltic States could not be left to the latter's own discretion. According to the later Soviet thesis, the Western Powers were trying "to drown the major issues in a swamp of minor amendments and innumerable versions," knowing full well that these would be unacceptable to Moscow. The same Soviet account reports that on May 27, 1939, Molotov told the British and French representatives that their countries seemed less interested in the pact than in talk about the pact. A few days later (May 31, 1939), the Foreign Commissar addressed the Supreme Soviet and reported on the negotiations. He voiced his suspicion that the Western Powers were not yet ready to abandon the policy of nonresistance to aggression, or at best were prepared only to resist in certain regions so as to divert the aggressor to other quarters. He then restated the Soviet demands and described them as absolutely minimal. In concluding he reminded his listeners (and indirectly the British and French) that the Moscow Government had no intention of renouncing business ties with other countries: trade discussions with the Germans had taken place in the early spring and they would probably be resumed.

This speech came to the British public and Government like a cold and disagreeable douche. Mr. Chamberlain, who no doubt felt that he had made a great concession, had announced on May 24, 1939, that he hoped for agreement within ten days and had thereby evoked tremendous popular enthusiasm. Now there was nothing to show but a prospect of Nazi-Soviet understanding. The disillusioned public was filled with misgivings and already began to fear lest Stalin sell out to the highest bidder.

But the issue was now fairly joined. Clearly the Soviet Government would not adhere to the peace front unless Britain and France, as well as Russia, guaranteed the independence of the Baltic States, along with Poland and Rumania. On its face this seemed a reasonable proposition, but it understandably confirmed the British Government in its conviction that the Kremlin had designs on these lost territories and that, if it chose to conclude that their independence was threatened by Germany, it would proceed to occupy them militarily. As matters stood at the beginning of June, 1939, they were well summed up in a State Department memorandum:

The question, therefore, presents itself as to whether the demands are made [by the Soviet Government] for the purpose of gaining greater security, or in order to effect a breakdown in the negotiations which would result in the Soviet Union being able, for an indefinite period, to play off the so-called democratic block against the Axis.

Much criticism was at the time and later leveled at Mr. Chamberlain for his inept handling of the negotiations with Moscow.

They were, in fact, marked by unwillingness and hesitation and showed little trace of clarity in conception or planning. But if British policy was maladroit, it seems reasonably clear that Soviet policy was dishonest. Once again it must be said that final proof is impossible. Nonetheless it appears almost certain that if Stalin meant to conclude an agreement with the democracies at all, it was only on the basis that Soviet Russia be given what amounted to a free hand in the Baltic States and Finland. Assuming that Soviet leaders did not expect Britain to make such a concession, one is forced to the conclusion that the chief purpose of the negotiations, from the Soviet standpoint, was to use them as a lever to move the Germans. The first discussions between Moscow and Berlin, in April and May, 1939, tend to support that thesis. . . . No doubt there were others who saw the advantages to the Nazis of a coalition with the detested Communists, but it seems that Hitler himself was reluctant to change his ideas or his plans. It may well be that the ideological aspect troubled him more than his lieutenants, and that he had doubts of his ability to convert his fanatical followers. Furthermore, he was probably loath to sacrifice his designs on Soviet territory. And finally, the Fuehrer seems to have been almost as distrustful of the Soviet Government as was Chamberlain. He had to ask himself whether the Kremlin was not plotting to involve Germany in war with the West and whether the Soviets might not make use of the negotiations to disillusion the Japanese about the German connection.

For a time Hitler hesitated and awaited developments. But by the end of May, 1939, the Germans had decided that the negotiations of the Western Powers with Soviet Russia might prove successful. To forestall such an eventuality it was thought wise to let the Kremlin know that Berlin was not uninterested in its suggestions. On May 30, 1939, State Secretary Weizsäcker, on instructions from Ribbentrop, broached the matter to Astakhov. He expressed agreement with Molotov's contention that economic and political affairs could not be kept entirely distinct, but indicated that German policy would be governed by the course of Soviet negotiations with other powers. In the most discreet way he called attention to the fact that the development of German-Polish relations had freed German policy in the East, and finally came to the main point. To quote his own record:

I did not know whether there still was any room at all for a possible gradual normalization of relations between Soviet Russia and Germany, now that Moscow had perhaps already listened to the enticements of London. At any rate, however, since the Chargé and his Ambassador had talked so frankly in the Foreign Ministry, I would like to spare myself the reproach that we ask anything from Moscow; we did not desire anything from Moscow, but neither did we want to be told by Moscow at a later date that we had erected between us an impenetrable wall of silence.

Apparently some expression of German interest was all that the Kremlin wanted for the time being. Even on the assumption that the Soviet leaders were more intent on an agreement with Germany than on anything else, it was patently to their interest to strike a bargain on the best possible terms. If Nazi uneasiness over the discussions between London, Paris and Moscow could be further stimulated, Hitler might in the end pay a high price for a pact. Whether or not this was Stalin's reasoning, he made no further advances to Germany during June and most of July, 1939, but on the contrary awaited the next moves of the Nazis. The Germans, badly in need of raw materials for war purposes, were quite ready to reopen trade negotiations and offered to send one of their experts to Moscow for the purpose. But the Soviet Commissar for Foreign Trade intimated that certain political questions would first have to be considered and in general gave the German Ambassador the impression that the Russians suspected Berlin of wanting to make political capital out of any further trade discussions. By the end of June, 1939,

the German Foreign Office was beginning to despair of progress along strictly economic lines. And yet, as the Nazi leaders pressed forward with their military plans against Poland, it became increasingly clear to them that an understanding with Moscow was essential.

On June 29, 1939, Count Schulenburg, returning to Moscow after extended conferences in Berlin, had a second interview with Molotov, during which the Ambassador made a concerted effort to open up the larger problem. He told the Soviet Commissar that Germany would welcome a "normalization" of relations and mentioned, as proof that Hitler had no hostile plans against the Soviets, the reserve shown by the German press, the conclusion of non-aggression pacts between Germany, Estonia and Latvia, and the continuing German desire to resume trade negotiations. To complete his argument he recalled that the German-Soviet treaty of friendship and nonaggression of 1926 was still in force.

Molotov listened attentively and voiced his satisfaction. The Soviet Government, he remarked, aimed at the cultivation of good relations with all its neighbors, but of course only on the basis of reciprocity. Becoming more pointed, he confessed that the Kremlin had had doubts of the validity of the treaty of 1926 in view of the hostile attitude of the Nazi Government and added acidly that with respect to the German nonaggression pacts with the Baltic States, "Germany had concluded them in her own interest, and not out of love for the Soviet Union." Furthermore, he queried the value of such agreements, considering Poland's recent experience with the German-Polish pact of 1934. It was exceedingly rare for German diplomats in the heyday of Nazi power to have to listen to such comments. Schulenburg was unable to hold out much hope to his Government. He was much impressed with Molotov's distrust of Germany, though he believed the Russians were interested in discovering Germany's desires and in maintaining contact with Berlin.

The German Foreign Office was baffled and irritated by Molotov's coolness. For the time being the Ambassador at Moscow was instructed to do nothing more. The Nazi leaders became ever more firmly convinced that the British-French-Soviet negotiations would succeed, yet they could not decide how to parry that blow. In the words of one Nazi official: "We could not drag Molotov and Mikoyan to Berlin through the Brandenburg Gate." Matters remained at dead center until suddenly, on July 22, 1939, the Soviet press announced that trade talks with the Germans would be resumed at Berlin. Apparently the Germans were surprised by this abrupt change, but agreeably so. A telegram was hastily sent to the German Embassy at Moscow stating that the Berlin Government was prepared to make substantial concessions because it desired a trade agreement for broader reasons. The Ambassador was told that the period of watchful waiting was over and that he might spin the thread of negotiation on. As of this date, then, the Nazis began to cast aside their reserve and systematically to pursue their objective.

While, during June and July, 1939, the Kremlin did little or nothing to encourage the Germans, it continued to negotiate actively with Britain and France, without, however, making much progress. The Soviet reply to the British-French note brought the prevalent optimism of London and Paris to an abrupt end (June 2, 1939), for the Moscow Government insisted not only that all reference to the League be omitted, but also that direct guarantees of the independence of Finland, Estonia and Latvia, as well as of Poland, Rumania, Turkey, Greece and Belgium, be written into the projected agreement. In addition, the Soviets now demanded that the political pact become effective only after the conclusion of a military convention.

Even the sanguine and impatient French statesmen were shocked by the exorbitance of the Soviet demand. They bemoaned the fact that the negotiations had been so badly bungled and blamed the British for having rejected the original Soviet proposal. Now, they argued, things had progressed to the point where the Kremlin recognized that its support was indispensable to the democracies. The Paris Government still wanted the pact with Russia and refused to give up hope of it. On the other hand, it had got wind of the Soviet notes to Estonia and Latvia and was simply appalled by their implications. According to French intelligence the Kremlin had informed the Estonian Government that the Soviet Union had an interest in preventing any other power from securing special political, military or economic privileges in that country and was therefore determined to defend Estonia against any such "aggression," whether Estonia requested aid or not. To French minds this left no doubt that Soviet armies might march into neighboring states at any time on the pretext of having to "protect" them. Under the terms laid down in the Soviet note of June 2, 1939, Britain and France would, in such a case, be called upon to support the Soviet action. To quote M. Bonnet: "France and England could certainly not consent to giving the Soviet Union support for such an extension of Bolshevism in Eastern Europe. . . . Acceptance of the Soviet proposal would mean consent to the establishment of a Soviet protectorate over the states named in the note."

If the French, who had previously been willing to guarantee the Baltic States, reacted in this fashion, the feelings aroused by the Soviet note in British Governmment circles can easily be imagined. Lord Halifax remarked that the Kremlin was taking the Western Powers "up a very dark road," while Mr. Chamberlain was so completely disillusioned that he questioned whether the Soviets had even the slightest intention of concluding a pact with the West. He would, so he said, make some concessions, but if they, too, failed to satisfy, he would be tempted to call the whole thing off. Apparently the Soviet demands induced in Chamberlain and some of his associates a relapse into the mentality of appeasement. Both the Prime Minister and the Foreign Secretary, replying in public to Hitler's repeated charges of encirclement, again expressed their abhorrence of a division of Europe into potentially hostile camps and reiterated their complete readiness to consider German needs and claims, once an atmosphere of peace and confidence had been restored. The German Ambassador in London, intent on forestalling a hostile coalition against his country, exerted himself to the utmost to convert British statesmen to the idea of direct conversations with the Nazi Government.

The problem of the Baltic States presented an almost insuperable obstacle to the success of the negotiations for a peace front. It seems reasonably clear that the Kremlin was genuinely apprehensive of German designs in that quarter. In Moscow the Finnish Government was regarded as anti-Soviet if not actually pro-German; indeed, that government was suspected of pressing for the refortification of the Åland Islands at the behest of Berlin. Nothing could dispel Soviet distrust, and at the end of June, 1939, the Kremlin notified the Finns that the Soviet Union could not agree to the refortification unless it were permitted to participate in the work on the same basis as Sweden. It is almost superfluous to add that the conclusion of non-aggression pacts between Germany, Estonia and Latvia served only to enhance Soviet suspicions and fears.

But for all that, there was more than sufficient reason for believing that the Soviet Government had territorial ambitions with regard to the entire frontier region lost to it in 1917 and the succeeding years. London and Paris were well aware of Soviet claims and hopes and therefore found themselves in an awkward if not impossible position when confronted with the Soviet note of June 2, 1939. Apart from their unwillingness to aid and abet the expansion of Communist power, they felt strongly that, after posing as the defenders of small states against aggression, they

could hardly themselves take part in forcing upon the Baltic States arrangements which they definitely did not want and would not accept. Like Poland and Rumania, all these countries objected violently to a Soviet guarantee or indeed to any guarantee that would seem to align them with one or another of the opposing European blocs. Hardly had their Governments realized what was being proposed when they announced publicly and privately that they desired to remain neutral and that they would resist all efforts to invade or occupy them. Privately they let it be known that if the British-French-Soviet negotiations eventuated in such guarantees, Estonia and Finland would conclude a military alliance against Russia and might even call in the Germans, who, in the last analysis, were preferable to the Russians.

Disheartened though the British Cabinet may have been, it felt impelled to seek a solution, partly because of the growing conviction of the Soviets' importance and partly because of the continued needling of the opposition. Churchill, for one, demanded action and wrote in the *New York Herald Tribune* (June 7, 1939):

Agreement is driven forward by irresistible forces overriding and shearing away serious obstacles and valid prejudices as if they were but straws. Personally . . . I have from the beginning preferred the Russian proposals to either the British or French alternatives. They are simple, they are logical and they conform to the main groupings of common interest.

Why not guarantee the Baltic States? he queried. If the Germans invaded those states, Poland would have to fight. So would Russia and the Western Powers. Why, then, not declare the fact?

In view of the grave questions at issue, the London Government might have been well advised to send Lord Halifax to Moscow, as some suggested. But Mr. Chamberlain would not even accept Mr. Eden's offer to undertake the mission, and finally named Sir William Strang, at that time Chief of the Central European Division of the Foreign Office, to assist Sir William Seeds, the ailing Ambassador at Moscow. The Soviets were to complain later that this was to foist off on them a subordinate and politically unimportant official. They scornfully recalled that Mr. Chamberlain had personally betaken himself to Hitler and maintained that at least Halifax might have come to Moscow.

Strang departed for Moscow in mid-June, 1939, bearing an assortment of proposals in the hope that at least one of them would prove palatable to the Kremlin. After prolonged discussions with his French colleague, he finally proposed to the Soviets that each of the three signatory powers should come to each other's assistance not only in case of direct aggression against any one of them, but also in the event of any one of them becoming involved in war on account of assistance against aggression afforded any state or states which any one of the signatories considered vital to its security. Aggression was defined as the crossing of frontiers with military forces. The states in question were not to be publicly named, but might be secretly listed. In return for this veiled guarantee of the Baltic States, the Western Powers requested that the Soviets guarantee Belgium, the Netherlands and Switzerland.

Prone though they were to criticize the British Government's attitude toward Russia, the French had to admit that their colleagues had "fallen over" themselves in agreeing to some form of guarantee for the Baltic States. Yet the Kremlin professed to remain dissatisfied. On June 29, 1939, the official newspaper *Pravda* published an astounding article by Andrei Zhdanov, a member of the all-powerful Politburo. The author's statement that he was expressing merely a personal opinion was given as little credit as it deserved and the article was therefore taken as an official utterance. According to Zhdanov the purpose of the British and French might be other than the construction of a peace front, the suggestion being that Moscow suspected the British and French of using the threat of a triple alliance to frighten Hitler into a new deal. Since the Western Governments entertained exactly the same misgivings about the Soviets, it is clear that the chances for a meeting of minds were slight.

Molotov, who had been conferring with the German Ambassador on the very day of the appearance of the Zhdanov article, lost little time in commenting on the latest British-French proposals. On July 4, 1939, he declared the veiled guarantee of the Baltic States inadequate and insisted that the guarantee should provide for cases of indirect as well as direct aggression. He indicated in this connection that Soviet Russia would take immediate action if a change of government in a Baltic State seemed to favor an aggressor. As for other items, the Commissar objected that the Soviets could not guarantee countries like the Netherlands and Switzerland, which had not even recognized the Soviet Government. At any rate, the Kremlin could not consider this question until it had concluded suitable pacts with Poland and Turkey. In conclusion, Molotov renewed his demand that the political agreement between the three Governments be made conditional on the prior signature of the proper military arrangements.

London and Paris were alike disheartened by the constant enlargement of the Soviet terms. They would never, so they said, accept a definition of indirect aggression that would permit the Soviets to march into the Baltic States at their pleasure, nor would they agree to make the political accord dependent on military discussions which might take months of time and even then fail of success. But the French Government was much disturbed by reports that Hitler meant to take action against Poland in August, 1939, and that he would do his utmost first to neutralize Soviet Russia by striking a bargain with Stalin. M. Bonnet therefore renewed his efforts to induce the British to yield further. British public opinion aided him in his campaign, for demands were already being made on Mr. Chamberlain to include Mr. Churchill in his Cabinet. The Prime Minister was utterly unwilling to entertain such notions, for he had no use for the policy urged by the opposition and was furthermore convinced that Mr. Churchill could not deliver one tenth of what the public expected of him; on the contrary, his presence in the Cabinet would only make for war.

The debate between London and Paris, and the concurrent discussions in Moscow, continued for fully three weeks. Eventually the British gave in on a number of points, excepting, however, the important matter of defining indirect aggression. They proposed that this be taken to mean an act which a guaranteed state might be forced to accept under threat and which might destroy its neutrality or jeopardize its independence. This, declared the British, was to be their last word. Their Ambassador to Moscow was instructed to make clear to Molotov that London's patience was running out and that it could not go on forever accepting endlessly increasing demands by the Kremlin.

At this juncture, as though to save a situation that was rapidly getting out of hand, Molotov on July 24, 1939, suddenly and surprisingly announced that the Soviet Government was satisfied. Substantial agreement, he said, had already been reached, for the differences with respect to indirect aggression were merely matters of nuance. There was no reason why military negotiations should not be initiated, so that both the political and military accords could be signed in the near future. The Commissar, indeed, accepted informally a draft agreement, of which the text has since been published. This draft reveals that the Moscow Government agreed to the retention of some mention of the League of Nations and accepted the British definition of indirect aggression as a basis for discussion. Furthermore, the Kremlin conceded that the political accord should become operative as soon as military arrangements were completed. British and French military missions were to be despatched to Moscow for this purpose. The guaranteed states,

listed in a secret protocol, were to be Estonia, Latvia, Lithuania, Poland, Rumania, Turkey, Greece and Belgium.

In London and Paris Molotov's unexpected tractability was taken to mean that the Soviets were really determined to sign a pact and that therefore the military negotiations could be wound up in a week or two. On July 27, 1939, it was publicly announced that special French and British military missions would depart for Moscow in the immediate future. The British public was jubilant. The long and arduous debates were seemingly at an end and the much-desired peace front appeared about to become a reality. After many nerve-racking months the heavens were clearing and the future once more took on a rosy hue.

However, in reviewing Molotov's extraordinary volte-face in the light of later developments it is hard to interpret it as anything but a cunning move in the Kremlin's complicated game of playing off the British and French against the Germans. On the assumption that the real objective of the Soviets was to strike a deal with the Germans that would enable them to keep out of a European conflict while at the same time furthering their own aims and interests in Eastern Europe, it was clearly advantageous for them to delude the Germans into thinking that they were about to join the front against aggression. Their purpose then must have been to prolong the discussions with the Western Powers as long as the situation seemed to require. During July, 1939, however, the negotiations had reached the point where there was danger of their breaking down. Thereupon Molotov, having tried the British almost beyond endurance, suddenly reversed himself and ostensibly agreed to their proposals in order to gain time.

It is altogether probable that during July, 1939, another factor entered into the Soviet calculations. About the middle of the month a German official of Goering's economic staff, Dr. Helmuth Wohltat, arrived in London to attend a whaling conference.

He was approached almost at once by Sir Horace Wilson, the confidential adviser of the Prime Minister, and Mr. Robert Hudson, Secretary for Overseas Trade, both of them gentlemen to whom Nazi proclivities were attributed. They discussed with Wohltat proposals which, they said, had the approval of the Prime Minister, and spoke freely of a British-German nonaggression pact which would enable the British Government to rid itself of its commitments to Poland. It is unnecessary to examine these advances in detail, but there seems to be no question of their authenticity. Mr. Chamberlain, who was never happy about the guarantee to Poland and who was definitely averse to the negotiations with Russia, was, informally and without the support of the Foreign Office, feeling out the Germans with a view to reviving the appeasement policy.

News of these doings soon leaked to the press, which printed distorted stories of a projected British loan of one billion pounds to Nazi Germany in order to enable that country to return to a peacetime economy. Actually the German Government showed no interest whatever in the British advances, but to the Kremlin, ever suspicious of Chamberlain's attachment to appeasement, it must have seemed that Britain and Germany were about to strike a bargain, perhaps at the expense of the Soviet Union as well as of Poland. . . .

Unfortunately for the Germans, the Russians were in no particular hurry, finding themselves in the enviable position of being wooed from all sides. Ribbentrop tried his hand with Astakhov on the evening of August 2, but made no progress. On August 3 Schulenburg had his all-important talk with Molotov. He found the dour Commissar somewhat less reserved than usual, but by no means tractable. In reply to the German suggestions he expressed some interest. In fact, he admitted that the Kremlin desired an improvement in relations. But he was pointed in his comments on past Nazi policy, especially its encouragement of Japan. With respect

to Soviet negotiations with the West he remarked that "The present course taken by the Soviet Union aimed at purely defensive ends and at the strengthening of a defensive front against aggression. In contrast to this, Germany had supported and promoted the aggressive attitude of Japan by the Anti-Comintern Pact and in the military alliance with Italy was pursuing offensive as well as defensive aims." The Ambassador felt obliged to report to his Government his impression "that the Soviet Government is at present determined to sign with England and France if they fulfill all Soviet wishes." To a friend he wrote a little more optimistically: "I believe that we put a few good fleas in the ears of the Soviets, anyhow. At every word and at every step one can see the great distrust toward us."

For another ten days the Germans tried in vain to induce Molotov to specify Soviet interests in the Baltic States and in Poland, which the Germans had expressed readiness to respect. Finally, on August 12, 1939, Astakhov was instructed to state the Kremlin's willingness to discuss various problems, but only by degrees or stages. The Russians proposed that the conversations take place in Moscow, but left open the question whether the Germans should send a special negotiator. On the strength of this exciting news Hitler told Ciano on the same day: "In the last few days there has been a Russian request for the despatch of a German plenipotentiary to Moscow to negotiate the friendship pact." The Fuehrer had suddenly become convinced that "the sending of the Anglo-French military mission to Moscow had only one purpose, i.e. to conceal the catastrophic position of the political negotiations."

Although it will be necessary at some later point to examine the validity of this last assertion of Hitler's, it is advisable, in the interests of clarity, to pursue the story of the Nazi-Soviet negotiations a little further before turning to other aspects of the situation. On August 14 Schulenburg was directed to see Molotov again and to restate the German position at length. The urgency of the matter was heavily underlined. The Ambassador was to say that Ribbentrop himself could come to Moscow with full powers to settle outstanding issues in short order, but that an extended conference between Schulenburg and Stalin would be a prerequisite for such a trip.

Hitler and his Foreign Minister waited at Berchtesgaden on pins and needles while Schulenburg conferred at length with Molotov on the evening of August 15. The Soviet Commissar was "unusually compliant and candid." He expressed himself as much gratified by the clear statement of the German program and professed to recognize the need for prompt action. On the other hand, he thought the visit of Ribbentrop would have to be carefully prepared and that therefore some time would be required. The Soviet Government would have to know first whether the Berlin Government saw any real possibility of influencing Japan in the direction of better relations with the Soviet Union, whether Germany would agree to a nonaggression pact with Russia, and whether Germany would contemplate a joint guarantee of the Baltic States. All these things, he opined, could be better handled in the first instance through regular diplomatic channels. The suggestion of a conference between the Ambassador and Stalin was passed over in silence.

In this interview of August 15 Molotov had, for the first time, indicated the Soviet desiderata. In the form he used they appeared modest and innocuous. Ribbentrop therefore cabled back at once, suggesting a twenty-five-year nonaggression pact, a suitable démarche in Tokyo and the proposed joint guarantee of the Baltic States. But the burden of his message dealt with his projected journey to the Soviet capital. Schulenburg was to say that Germany was determined not to endure Polish provocation indefinitely and that "serious incidents" might occur any day. He was to propose to Molotov that the visit take place within a few days.

There was, however, no hurrying the Soviet Commissar. On August 17 he handed Schulenburg the formal reply of the Kremlin to the proposals of August 15. This document began with yet another rehearsal of past Soviet grievances and then outlined the following procedure: first, conclusion of the economic accord; second, signature of a nonaggression pact or reaffirmation of the neutrality treaty of 1926; third, simultaneously with the nonaggression pact, conclusion of "a special protocol which would define the interests of the signatory parties in this or that question of foreign policy and which would form an integral part of the pact." Molotov suggested that the Germans try their hand at drafting these agreements. As for the projected Ribbentrop visit, he remarked that the practical work could be done without much ceremony and that the Kremlin did not like the publicity attaching to such a visit.

Champing at the bit as the date for the attack on Poland drew near, Hitler agreed to everything. The trade discussions were hastily concluded on August 18 and a draft nonaggression treaty was despatched at once to Moscow. The Ambassador was to remind Molotov again that German-Polish relations were becoming more acute from day to day and might make the outbreak of hostilities unavoidable. A "historic turning point" had been reached and the Ribbentrop visit should take place as soon as humanly possible. But Molotov remained unmoved. He insisted that time was required to study the terms of a political agreement and submitted his own draft of a nonaggression pact, to run for only five years. Only after what the German Ambassador conjectured must have been intervention on Stalin's part did the Foreign Commissar agree that Ribbentrop might come to Moscow on August 26 or 27, provided the conclusion of the economic agreement were published at once.

By ordinary standards the discussions were progressing not only at a reasonable but at an unusually rapid rate. But for

Hitler every day counted. On August 20 he sent a personal message addressed to Mr. J. V. Stalin, Moscow, concurring in everything and urging that, because the tension between Germany and Poland had become "intolerable," Ribbentrop be received on August 22 or at the latest on August 23 to sign the nonaggression pact and the secret protocol. This telegram was handed to Molotov on the afternoon of August 21 and Stalin replied at once in a message "to the Chancellor of the German Reich, A. Hitler." The Soviet leader raised no further objection and consented to Ribbentrop's arrival on August 23. Molotov informed the German Ambassador that the Soviet Government would like Hitler's concurrence in the publication next morning of a communiqué announcing the coming conclusion of the nonaggression pact and the projected visit of Ribbentrop. This was given at once.

Soviet acceptance of the Ribbentrop visit brought the maneuvering to an end and provides a convenient opportunity for review and summary of the Nazi-Soviet relationship. Although by August 12, 1939, the Soviet decision for a deal with Hitler had certainly been made, the Kremlin continued to temporize for another ten days. Stalin and Molotov were obviously making every effort to prolong the discussions and to postpone the Ribbentrop visit as long as they dared. Their main preoccupations at this time seem to have been with alleviation of the tension in Soviet relations with Japan and with the attainment of Soviet objectives in the Baltic States. Constant German references to the Polish problem and reiterated expressions of readiness to take account of Soviet interests in Poland elicited almost no response. Molotov hardly brushed this question, though he must have been as aware as anyone of the acute danger of a German-Polish clash. One is tempted to believe that at first Stalin and Molotov were envisaging a pact much less profitable to them than the agreement presently to be concluded. Only when they began to realize that Hitler felt unable to

act against Poland without a pact with Russia did they see the possibility of securing a secret protocol involving much more extensive political settlements. In this connection it is worth noting that when Ribbentrop landed at the Moscow airfield he still had no clear idea of the prospective Soviet demands. The Germans were prepared for concessions in the entire area from the Baltic to the Black Sea. The Kremlin was in the position to make the most of the situation. Once Ribbentrop had openly committed himself to the pact, he could hardly reject even the most extravagant demands. However, before Stalin could close with Ribbentrop, he had to dispose of the British-French military missions, of whose sad fate something must now be said.

The British and French military missions arrived in the Soviet capital on August 11, 1939, just as the conversations between Russia and Germany were entering upon their crucial stage. The French mission was led by an able staff officer, General Joseph Doumenc, but the British, strangely enough, was headed by a naval officer, who, even if able, could hardly have hoped to impress the Russians. . . .

The Kremlin had appointed its highest military authority, General Klimenty Voroshilov, the Chief of Staff, to conduct the discussions on the Soviet side. Voroshilov received the foreign missions with much pomp and circumstance and the meetings opened on August 12–13, 1939, in an atmosphere of warm cordiality which left the French convinced that the Russians meant business. To be sure, the Soviet chief was disappointed to learn that Admiral Plunkett and General Doumenc were authorized only to negotiate, but he agreed that a start should be made by having each delegation provide a statement of its country's military capabilities. The British and French did so, confessing in the process that the Polish Army, unless heavily supplied, could not last long. To this Voroshilov replied by raising the question of how the Soviets could aid. On August 14 he answered his own query by stating categorically:

. . . that the first condition for Soviet military coöperation with France and England was that the Polish Government should announce to the Soviet Government its willingness to permit the Red Army to enter Poland by way of Vilna in the North and by way of Lemberg on the South for the purpose of combatting the German armies in case France, England and Poland should become involved in war with Germany.

According to their instructions, the British and French negotiators urged that the Soviet Government take up this matter directly with Warsaw and Bucharest. In any event, they said, this was a political question which they would have to refer to their Governments. General Doumenc made heroic efforts to persuade Voroshilov to continue the talks without reference to the problem of passage, but the Soviet general stood his ground. Probably in order to impress his hearers with the strength of the Soviet position, he stated on August 15 that the Russians were prepared to put 120 infantry and sixteen cavalry divisions into the field, and that they had 5000 planes.

The cards were now on the table. The British and French were squarely faced with the ever-recurring problem of the passage of Soviet troops through Polish territory. The Soviet Government, as noted above, raised the question why the London and Paris Governments had not settled this issue before sending the military missions to Moscow. The answer is not easy, but part of it rests on the fact, clearly expressed in the instructions to the missions, that the British and French held very definite views on the military situation in Eastern Europe. They had a poor opinion of the Soviet Army and therefore put little store by its active participation. On the other hand they believed that the Polish Army, if given adequate equipment and supplies, would be a first-rate fighting force. Therefore all they desired of the Russians was the provision of needed matériel to the Poles. The Soviet insistence on doing more than they contemplated was a matter of grave embarrassment to the British and French.

Certain other aspects of the Polish problem undoubtedly influenced the situation also. In May, 1939, a Polish military mission had visited Paris and had proposed the conclusion of a political-military agreement to supplement the existing guarantee. With much reluctance the French General Staff had consented to arrangements which assured the Poles that within sixteen days of the outbreak of hostilities the French Army would launch a major attack on the German frontier. But at the last moment Foreign Minister Bonnet refused to sign the complementary political agreement, on the plea that the British had not yet done likewise. It seems likely that Bonnet had convinced himself that the Germans would make war, if necessary, to gain their objectives in Danzig, and that he therefore wished to avoid any accord which involved recognition of any change in the status of Danzig as a legitimate cause for Poland's going to war. The details are still obscure, but the end result of his imbroglio was much irritation with Bonnet in French Government circles and violent recriminations between the Polish Ambassador and the French Foreign Minister.

The British were hardly more successful in their efforts to grapple with the Polish problem. A military mission had been sent to Warsaw in late May, 1939, and had reported fully on Poland's serious shortages in equipment and supplies. Thereupon the Poles began negotiations in London for a credit and a loan. Apparently British financial circles were chary about further large investments. The Poles, indeed, had the feeling that they still cherished hopes of a deal with Hitler. More important, however, was the fact that Britain was already under heavy financial strain, that Britain needed for its own use the very military items which Poland required, and that a loan threatened too great a drain on gold reserves. The discussions dragged on for weeks and eventuated, on August 2, 1939, in a credit agreement in the sum of eight million pounds, the French extending a comparable credit. Actually, however, practically no equipment reached Poland from Britain prior to the outbreak of war. The military agreement between the two countries had been deferred pending the financial negotiations, and was not finally concluded until August 25, 1939. Clearly there were real difficulties in the way of implementing the guarantee extended to Poland in March, 1939, but it is not surprising that Hitler regarded the endless delays on the part of the British as evidence that they did not intend to take their guarantees seriously.

There is no reason to believe that after the discussions of March, 1939, either the British or the French made efforts to induce the Poles to agree to the passage of Soviet troops. The attitude of Warsaw was well known and, as aforesaid, it was thought that Russian aid in the form of supplies was all that would be necessary. Voroshilov's uncompromising demand on August 14 therefore struck like a bombshell. Nonetheless, General Doumenc considered the Soviet demand justified and took it to mean that the Kremlin did not intend to "remain on the balcony," but really to get into the fight. He asked and received permission from Paris to send an emissary to Warsaw in the effort to convert the Polish General Staff. Meanwhile Bonnet raised the issue with the Polish Ambassador as a matter of greatest urgency, and the British and French Military Attachés in Warsaw were instructed from home to bring pressure on the Polish High Command. But the Poles refused to yield. Foreign Minister Beck expressed doubt whether the Germans would make war, at least before the end of September, and asserted his country's ability to resist. Threats of a Nazi-Soviet pact left him unmoved. The Soviet demand for passage of troops, he said, "is nothing less than a new partition, which we are being asked to

subscribe to. If we are partitioned, we shall at least defend ourselves. There is nothing to guarantee us that the Russians, once they are installed in our country, will participate actively in the war." Marshal Rydz-Smigly voiced his sentiments even more bluntly: "With the Germans we risk losing our liberty; with the Russians we lose our soul." Hours were spent in argument, the French insisting that it would be utter folly to reject the Soviet offer of genuine military support and offering to send two French divisions to assist the Soviet forces. Again and again they assured the Poles that the French and British could get from the Kremlin absolute guarantees of eventual evacuation and that they would give Poland "absolute guarantees of those guarantees." Nothing would avail. By August 20 the Poles had made only one slight concession: Colonel Beck had agreed that the French mission at Moscow "might approve [passage of Soviet troops through Poland] as though no question had been put to Poland."

In retrospect one must sympathize with the Poles, headstrong though they may have been in some respects. There was no assurance that the Soviet armies, once they had moved into Poland, would actually engage the Nazis, and, with regard to the eventual withdrawal of the Russians, Polish apprehensions were surely not without foundation. Nevertheless, the French were infuriated with the Poles. Evidently M. Bonnet did not seriously question the good faith of the Soviet Government, while in Moscow the French Ambassador, M. Naggiar, pressed for a conclusion on any terms. On the other hand, the French Counselor of Embassy, M. Payart, put no trust whatever in the Russians and regarded the entire negotiation as a terrible hoax. His views were shared by other experienced diplomats in Moscow, but made no impression on his superiors.

Premier Daladier, taking full advantage of the opening suggested by Beck, on August 21, 1939, instructed General Doumenc to agree in principle to the passage of Soviet troops through the Vilna and Lemberg corridors. At the same time both chiefs of mission were sent full powers to conclude the military convention. On the very next day they communicated these happy tidings to Voroshilov, but only to meet with a cool reception. The Soviet general was annoyingly scrupulous in analyzing the agreement regarding passage of Soviet troops. He wanted to know whether the British Government concurred in the French statement and whether the Governments of Warsaw and Bucharest had given their approval. Without such approval, he observed, nothing could be done. Remarking significantly that the British and French had dawdled so long that "certain political events" might intervene, the Soviet chief excused himself and went duck-shooting.

Events had indeed outrun the course of the military conversations. On August 20, 1939, had come the announcement of the conclusion of a Nazi-Soviet trade agreement. Then, on the evening of the eventful August 22, 1939, the Soviet press agency elucidated Voroshilov's cryptic utterance by reporting that Ribbentrop would arrive presently for the negotiation of a Nazi-Soviet nonaggression pact. The capitals of Europe reeled under the blow while Bonnet, in a last desperate move, appealed once more to Warsaw. On the afternoon of August 23, just as Ribbentrop arrived in Moscow, the Polish Government finally gave qualified consent to the French demand:

The Polish Government agrees that General Doumenc should make the following statement: "We have come to the conviction that in case of common action against German aggression, coöperation between Poland and the U.S.S.R. is not to be excluded (or is possible), under technical conditions to be determined. The British and French General Staffs consider that therefore all hypotheses of collaboration should be immediately studied.

There was little if any prospect that the exigent Russians would regard this evasive statement with favor. Voroshilov, when informed of this new turn, simply reiterated his previous stand and insisted that the British and French Governments guarantee the agreement of Warsaw and Bucharest.

Though further discussion had by this time become obviously futile, the Western Powers still grasped at straws. One of these was a statement by an official Soviet spokesman with reference to the forthcoming Ribbentrop visit: "We want to regularize commercial arrangements with Germany. We want to conclude a proper agreement with the democratic powers to restrain further aggression by the Fascist powers. We see nothing incompatible in the simultaneous pursuit of both aims." The British Ambassador called at once on Commissar Molotov and requested clarification of this statement. The ensuing conversation was plain-spoken on both sides. Sir William Seeds inquired about the nature of the proposed Nazi-Soviet pact and asked whether it would contain the so-called "escape clause," characteristic of Soviet nonaggression pacts with other countries, which would render the agreement inoperative if either party committed aggression against a third state. But Molotov was evasive: the official communiqué, he insisted, contained the facts and for the rest the British would have to "wait and see." In reply to the Ambassador's suggestion that the Kremlin was acting in bad faith, the Commissar disputed any British claim to sit in judgment on Soviet policy and reminded Sir William that he had repeatedly charged the British with complete insincerity. The height of this insincerity, he continued, had been reached when the military missions arrived without powers to discuss such basic issues as the passage of Soviet troops through Poland and Rumania. The Soviet Government had therefore been forced to the conclusion that it was being "diddled" and that it had best close with the Nazi offers. The Ambassador did his utmost to defend British-French policy and took the occasion to recall all the concessions that had been made to the Soviet viewpoint.

Molotov asserted that he had little interest in the past, yet closed with the suggestion that the military missions remain in Moscow until the outcome of the German-Soviet negotiations were known. That is, he invited the British and French to cool their heels at the door while Ribbentrop was being received within.

Molotov's contentions and the postwar Soviet apologia both show that from the outset the Soviet Government attempted to blame the British-French military missions for the breakdown of negotiations and for the conclusion of the spectacular Nazi-Soviet pact. Yet the merest comparison of dates disproves this thesis. The Kremlin had agreed with Berlin on August 12, 1939, that is, before the beginning of the military conversations, to discuss concrete political problems. Furthermore, Stalin had consented to Ribbentrop's visit before the British and French had made a final statement on the issue of the passage of Soviet troops through Polish or Rumanian territory. All the evidence indicates that the Soviet leaders desired the coming of the military missions partly to impress and soften the Germans and partly in order to keep the door ajar in case an agreement with Hitler proved impossible. By August 22 they certainly had reason to suppose that the Germans would pay dearly for a pact, yet even then Molotov made the strange suggestion that the missions remain until the Kremlin had made doubly sure of its prospective gains. Viewed in this light, the much discussed obduracy of the Poles in refusing assent to the passage of Soviet troops loses most of its significance. That issue was really nothing more than a convenient instrument by which the Soviet negotiators managed to protract the discussions. All in all, the Soviet policy in this latter phase was one of shameless deception.

August 22, 1939, was a red-letter day in the annals of even a career like Adolf Hitler's. Having heard that Stalin was prepared to receive Ribbentrop and conclude a nonaggression pact, the Fuehrer felt completely free to loose the attack on Poland, scheduled for the morning of August 26. In great elation he summoned his generals to a conference at Obersalzberg. Though there are disparities among the records of his remarks, the general tenor and content of the various versions are the same. They leave no doubt that the session was one of the most extraordinary and dramatic of all history. The Fuehrer began by recalling his original plan to attack the West in two or three years. This plan, he said, had been abandoned when, in the spring of 1939, it became clear that Poland could not be trusted at Germany's rear and therefore would first have to be liquidated. The Nazi dictator pointed out that time pressed since the German economic situation was deteriorating. Besides, he added, with exuberant self-conceit, the future depended so much upon himself? "Probably no one will ever again have the confidence of the whole German people as I do. There will probably never again be a man with more authority than I have. My existence is therefore a factor of great value. But I might be eliminated at any time by some criminal or idiot." The same, in lesser degree, was true of Mussolini and Franco. By contrast neither Britain nor France had the leadership to enable them to embark on a long life-and-death struggle: "Our enemies are little worms. I saw them at Munich." Britain and France were in decline and their much vaunted rearmament did not as yet amount to much. Germany therefore had much to gain and little to lose. The probability was great that the Western Powers would not interfere. In any case, Germany must accept the risk and act with reckless resolution.

At this point the Fuehrer broke the great news: the coming deal with Soviet Russia. Stalin, he declared, was one of the three great statesmen of the world: "Stalin and I are the only ones that see the future. So I shall shake hands with Stalin within a few weeks on the common German-Russian border and undertake with him a new distribution of the world." But, he hastened to add, this would be only a temporary expedient. (When the time came, the Soviet Union would be dealt with like Poland: "After Stalin's death (he is seriously ill), we shall crush the Soviet Union." However, for the moment the international situation was extraordinarily favorable. By the agreement with Russia the weapons of the democracies would be dashed from their hands and Poland would be maneuvered into the position needed for German success. Some propaganda reason could readily be found for starting the war) "The victor will not be asked later on whether he told the truth or not. In starting and waging war, not the Right is what matters, but the Victory." The struggle, he directed, was to be waged with the utmost brutality and the Poles were to be exterminated without mercy: "Only in this way will we win the living space that we need. . . . Eighty million people shall get what is their right. Their existence has to be secured. The strongest has the right." (His one great fear, concluded Hitler, was that at the last minute some "dirty dog" like Chamberlain would bring up proposals for mediation. In that case he would be kicked downstairs)

The notes taken by Hitler's listeners record that after this exultant outburst Goering led the cheering. He jumped upon the table and offered bloodthirsty thanks while he danced like a savage. Only a few doubtful officers remained silent. Perhaps some of the old-line soldiers had grave misgivings about the course of Nazi leadership. But the moment was hardly propitious for objection and protest. (Some undercover effort was made to forestall the fateful decision, but the key men of the Army refused to cooperate and plans for organized opposition had to be abandoned)

To what extent Hitler's bravado may have been designed to win over his uneasy generals one cannot say, but in any case his remarks provide an interesting if unedifying commentary on the negotiations of Ribbentrop in Moscow. The Foreign Minister reached the Soviet capital about noon on August 23, 1939, accompanied by a large staff. It seems likely that he expected long wrangling on details, but, as it turned out, his Foreign Office experts were not needed at all and only one of them, the legal adviser, took any part in the discussions. Ribbentrop had a long conference with Stalin and Molotov on the afternoon of his arrival. Almost nothing is known of the conversation, but Stalin inquired first of all whether the Germans were prepared to disinterest themselves in Estonia and Latvia to the extent of giving up claims to the seaports of Libau and Windau. This question was referred to Hitler by telephone and an affirmative reply was received that same evening. Ribbentrop came away from the first conference with the feeling that the hoped-for deal could be successfully arranged. In the evening the principals reassembled for a second session, lasting from 10 P.M. to 1 A.M. Stalin having been told of Hitler's compliance in the matter of the Baltic States, the atmosphere became warm and cordial. The agreement on the nonaggression pact presented little difficulty, save for the fact that Stalin objected to a flowery preamble celebrating Nazi-Soviet friendship. After all, he remarked, the Nazis had for years poured such "buckets of filth" upon the Soviet Government that the latter could hardly be expected publicly to proclaim its friendship. But this was by the by. (On matters of substance agreement was easy, for the Germans assented to everything. With regard to Japan, Stalin admitted that the Kremlin desired better relations, but made it clear that if Japan wanted war, it could have war. Ribbentrop offered to do what he could to eliminate friction, but Stalin — no doubt anticipating the effect of the Nazi-Soviet pact on Tokyo — was anxious to have it understood that his Government would not take the initiative. There was some discussion of the position of Italy and of Turkey, and both sides indulged in some caustic remarks about the weakness and presumption of Britain)

Turning then to the terms of the secret protocol, which was to be an integral part of the agreement, Ribbentrop left no doubt that the Germans would not put up with Polish "provocation" any longer. He and the Soviet chiefs thereupon proceeded to plan the partition of Poland, the respective spheres to be defined by the courses of the Pisa, Narew, Vistula and San Rivers. Finland, Estonia and Latvia, "in case of a politico-territorial change," were assigned to the Soviet sphere, and Lithuania to the German. The Soviet Government "emphasized" its interest in Bessarabia, and the Nazi envoy declared Germany's complete "political disinterestedness" in southeastern Europe. The agreements were signed at about 1 A.M. on August 24, though dated August 23, 1939. Stalin was elated and "did not hide from Ribbentrop the fact that he had long been in favor of a Soviet-German *rapprochement*." He drank a toast to Hitler and to "the revival of the traditional German-Russian friendship." Ribbentrop reciprocated. The "tremendous political overturn," as Hitler described it, had been accomplished. By noon next day Ribbentrop was able to report to the Fueher the details of his brilliant achievement at Moscow. . . .

SOVIET REBUTTAL: THE WEST DELIBERATELY APPEASED HITLER

Historians as well as artists in the Soviet Union must produce works that harmonize with the official attitude of the Communist leaders of the U.S.S.R. The official Soviet view of the coming of World War II, as presented in 1948 and reprinted below, gave Soviet historians the framework within which they must interpret the diplomacy of the 1930's, and at the same time served as Communist propaganda within and outside the Soviet Union. A massive, colorful, and tendentious three-volume Soviet publication of 1961 on the Second World War merely elaborated on the themes presented in this reading. While pre-1941 Soviet statements denounced British and French appeasement of Germany, Soviet accounts since 1948 have reflected the "Cold War" and the rise of the United States as the leader of the West by seeking to prove that American capitalists and governmental leaders stood behind the European appeasers in the 1930's in an attempt to encourage Nazi aggression against the U.S.S.R. Does this interpretation reflect only "Cold War" strategy? If it is solidly based on substantial evidence about American policy in the 1930's the United States bears a major responsibility for the outbreak of the Second World War.

At the end of January [1948], the State Department of the United States of America, in collaboration with the British and French Foreign Offices, published a collection of reports and various records from the diaries of Hitlerite diplomatic officials, under the mysterious title: "Nazi-Soviet Relations, 1939–1941."

As evident from the preface to this collection, as far back as the summer of 1946 the Governments of the United States of America, Great Britain and France had already agreed to publish archive materials of the German Foreign Office for 1918–1945, seized in Germany by American and British military authorities. Noteworthy in this connection is the fact that the published collection contains only material relating to the period of 1939–1941, while material relating to the preceding years, and in particular to the Munich period, has not been included by the Department of State in the collection and thus has been concealed from world public opinion. This action is certainly not accidental, but pursues aims which have nothing to do with an objective and honest treatment of historical truth. . . .

The collection is full of documents concocted by Hitlerite diplomatic officials in the depths of the German diplomatic offices. This fact alone should have served as a warning against unilateral use and publication of documents which are one-sided and tendentious, giving an account of events from the standpoint of the Hitler Government, and which are intended to present these events in a light which would be favorable to the Hitlerites. . . .

The American, British, and French Governments have unilaterally published the German documents without hesitating to falsify history in their efforts to slander the Soviet Union, which bore the brunt of the struggle against Hitlerite aggression.

By doing so, these Governments have as-

From *Falsificators of History* (*An Historical Note*) (Moscow, 1948), pp. 3, 5–7, 10–11, 16–25, 27–31, 36–38, 40–42, a publication of the Soviet Information Bureau.

sumed full responsibility for the consequences of this unilateral action.

In view of this, the Soviet Government on its part feels itself entitled to make public the secret documents concerning relations between Hitler Germany and the Governments of Great Britain, the United States of America and France which fell into the hands of the Soviet Government, and which the above-mentioned three Governments *concealed* from public opinion. . . .

American fakers and their British and French associates are trying to create the impression that the preparations for German aggression which developed into the Second World War were begun in the autumn of 1939. Yet who can swallow this bait nowadays but absolutely naive people prepared to believe any sensational fabrication?

Who does not know that Germany began preparing for war immediately after Hitler had come to power? Who does not know, moreover, that the Hitler regime was established by German monopoly circles with the full approval of the ruling camp of England, France and the United States?

In order to prepare for war and to provide herself with the most modern armament, Germany had to restore and develop her heavy industry, and first of all her metallurgical and war industries in the Ruhr. Having sustained defeat in the first imperialist war Germany, then under the yoke of the Versailles treaty, could not do this with her own forces in a short period. German imperialism was rendered powerful support in this matter by the United States of America.

Who does not know that in the post-Versailles period, American banks and trusts, acting in full accord with the Government, made investments in German economy and granted Germany credits running into billions of dollars, which were spent on reconstruction and development of the war industrial potential of Germany? . . .

It was this golden rain of American dollars that fertilized the heavy industry of Hitler Germany and in particular her war industry. It was billions of American dollars invested by overseas monopolies in the war economy of Hitler Germany that re-established Germany's war potential and placed in the hands of the Hitler regime the weapons it needed for aggression. . . .

Another factor of decisive importance which helped to unleash Hitler aggression was the policy of the ruling circles of England and France which is known as the policy of "appeasing" Hitler Germany, a policy of renouncing collective security. At present it should be clear to everyone that it was this policy of British and French ruling circles as expressed in their renunciation of collective security, in their refusal to resist German aggression, in their connivance with Hitler Germany's aggressive demands, that led to the Second World War. . . .

As far back as 1937, it became perfectly clear that a great war was being hatched by Hitler with the direct connivance of Great Britain and France. Documents of the German Foreign Ministry captured by Soviet troops after Germany's defeat reveal the true essence of Great Britain's and France's policy of the time. These documents show that, essentially, Anglo-French policy was aimed not at mustering the forces of the peace-loving states for a common struggle against aggression, but at isolating the USSR and directing the Hitlerite aggression toward the East, against the Soviet Union, at using Hitler as a tool for their own ends. . . .

The fact that the American Government undertook to make the German files public, while excluding the documents pertaining to the Munich agreement, shows that the United States Government is interested in whitewashing the heroes of the Munich treachery and in putting the blame on the USSR. The substance of Britain's and France's Munich policy was sufficiently clear even before this. Documents from the archives of the German Foreign Ministry, now at the disposal of the Soviet Government, furnish, however, abundant new data which reveal the true meaning of the prewar diplomacy of the Western Powers; they show how the destinies of nations were played with, how brazenly these Powers traded in other peoples' territories, how they had been secretly re-dividing the map of the world, how they encouraged Hitlerite aggression, and they show the efforts made to direct that aggression toward the East, against the Soviet Union.

This is eloquently borne out, for instance, by a German document recording a conversation which took place between Hitler and the British Minister, Halifax, in the presence of Von Neurath, the German Foreign Minister, in Obersalzberg on November 19, 1937. Halifax declared that

he (Lord Halifax) and the other members of the British Government were fully aware that the Fuehrer had attained a great deal, not only inside Germany herself, but that having destroyed Communism in his country, he had barred the road of the latter to Western Europe, and that therefore Germany was entitled to be regarded as the bulwark of the West against Bolshevism.

Speaking on behalf of the British Prime Minister, Chamberlain, Halifax pointed out that there was every possibility of finding a solution even of difficult problems if Germany and Britain could reach agreement with France and Italy too.

Halifax said that

there should not be an impression that the Berlin-Rome Axis, or that good relations between London and Paris, would suffer as a result of Anglo-German rapprochement. After the ground is prepared by Anglo-German rapprochement, the four great West-European Powers [i.e., Great Britain, France, Germany and Italy] must jointly set up the foundation for lasting peace in Europe. Under no conditions should any of the four Powers remain outside this co-operation, or else there would be no end to the present unstable situation.

In other words, Halifax, as far back as 1937, had proposed to Hitler on behalf of the British Government, that Britain as

well as France should join the Berlin-Rome Axis.

To this proposal, however, Hitler replied with a statement to the effect that such an agreement among the four Powers seemed to him very easy to arrange if good will and a kindly attitude prevailed, but that it would prove more difficult if Germany were not regarded "as a state which no longer carried the moral and material stigma of the Treaty of Versailles."

In reply to this, Halifax, according to the record, said:

"Britishers are realists and perhaps more than others are convinced that the errors of the Versailles dictate must be rectified. Britain has always exercised her influence in this realistic sense in the past." He pointed to Britain's role with regard to the evacuation of the Rhineland ahead of the time fixed, the settlement of the reparations problem, and the reoccupation of the Rhineland.

From the further record of Hitler's conversation with Halifax, it is evident that the British Government viewed favorably Hitler's plans for the "acquisition" of Danzig, Austria, and Czechoslovakia. Having discussed with Hitler the questions of disarmament and the League of Nations, and having noted that further discussion was needed, Halifax stated:

All other questions can be characterized as relating to changes in the European order, changes which sooner or later will probably take place. To these questions belong those of Danzig, Austria, and Czechoslovakia. England is only interested that these changes should be effected by peaceful evolution, so as to avoid methods which may cause further convulsions, undesired either by the Fuehrer or by other countries.

This conversation evidently was not the mere sounding out of an interlocutor, which sometimes is called for by political necessity; it was a deal, a secret agreement of the British Government with Hitler about satisfying the annexationist appetites of the latter at the expense of third countries. In this connection, the statement in Parliament of the British Minister Simon on February 21, 1938, is noteworthy. He said that Great Britain had never given special guarantees regarding the independence of Austria. This was a deliberate lie, because such guarantees were given by the Treaties of Versailles and St. Germain.

At the same time, British Prime Minister Chamberlain stated that Austria could not count upon any protection on the part of the League of Nations.

We must not try to delude ourselves, and still more, we must not try to delude small weak nations into thinking that they will be protected by the League against aggression and acting accordingly, when we know that nothing of the kind can be expected.

In this way the makers of British policy encouraged Hitler to annexationist actions. . . .

The next link in the chain of German aggression and the preparation of war in Europe was the seizure of Czechoslovakia by Germany. And this most important step in unleashing war in Europe could be taken by Hitler only with the direct support of England and France.

On July 10, 1938, Dirksen, the German Ambassador to London, reported to Berlin that for the British Government

one of the most essential planks of its program is to find a compromise with Germany, [and that] this Government displays with regard to Germany such a maximum of understanding as could be displayed by any of the likely combinations of British politicians.

Dirksen wrote that the British Government

has come nearer to understanding the most essential points of the main demands advanced by Germany; namely: to keep the Soviet Union out of deciding the destinies of Europe; likewise to keep out the League of Nations; as well as the advisability of bilateral negotiations and treaties.

Dirksen also reported to Berlin that the British Government was ready to make great sacrifices to "meet the other just demands of Germany."

Thus, between the British Government and Hitler there was indeed established a far-reaching accord on foreign policy plans, which fact Dirksen so lucidly reported to Berlin. It is not necessary to recall the universally known facts relating directly to the Munich deal. But one cannot forget that on September 19, 1938, i. e., four days after Hitler's meeting at Berchtesgaden with Chamberlain, who arrived for this purpose by plane, representatives of the British and French Governments demanded from the Czechoslovak Government the transfer to Germany of the Czechoslovak regions populated mainly by Sudeten Germans.

They maintained that if this demand were not complied with, it would be impossible to preserve peace and to secure the vital interests of Czechoslovakia.

The Anglo-French sponsors of Hitler's aggression attempted to cover their treachery with the promise of an international guarantee of the new frontiers of the Czechoslovak State as "a contribution to the pacification of Europe.". . .

At a conference of Hitler, Chamberlain, Mussolini, and Daladier held in Munich on September 29 and 30, 1938, the disgraceful deal, which had been completely agreed upon in advance among the chief participants in the conspiracy against the peace, was finally concluded. The fate of Czechoslovakia was decided behind her back. Representatives of Czechoslovakia were invited to Munich only meekly to await the results of the conspiracy of the imperialists. The entire conduct of Britain and France left no doubt that this unheard-of act of treachery on the part of the British and French Governments in regard to the Czechoslovak people and republic, far from being a chance episode in the policy of these States, represented a highly important phase in their policy aimed at goading the Hitlerite aggressors against the Soviet Union.

The true meaning of the Munich conspiracy was then exposed by J. V. Stalin who said that "the districts of Czechoslovakia were yielded to Germany as the price of undertaking to launch war on the Soviet Union."

The essence of that policy of the Anglo-French ruling circles of the time was exposed by J. V. Stalin at the Eighteenth Congress of the Communist Party of the Soviet Union (Bolsheviks), in March, 1939.

The policy of non-intervention means conniving at aggression, giving free rein to war, and consequently transforming the war into world war. The policy of non-intervention reveals an eagerness, a desire, not to hinder the aggressors in their nefarious work: not to hinder Japan, say, from embroiling herself in a war with China, or better still, with the Soviet Union; not to hinder Germany, say, from enmeshing herself in European affairs, from embroiling herself in a war with the Soviet Union; to allow all belligerents to sink deeply into the mire of war; to encourage them surreptitiously in this direction; to allow them to weaken and exhaust one another; and then, when they have become weak enough, to appear on the scene with fresh strength, to appear, of course, in "the interests of peace," and to dictate conditions to the enfeebled belligerents. . . .

Through all phases of the Czechoslovak drama, the Soviet Union alone of all the Great Powers vigorously championed the independence and national rights of Czechoslovakia. Seeking to justify themselves in the eyes of public opinion, the Governments of Great Britain and France hypocritically declared that they did not know whether or not the Soviet Union would live up to its pledges, given to Czechoslovakia in accordance with the treaty of mutual assistance. But this was a deliberate lie, for the Soviet Government had publicly declared its willingness to stand up for Czechoslovakia against Germany in accordance with the terms of that treaty, which called for simultaneous action on the part of France in defense of Czechoslovakia. France, however, refused to discharge her duty. . . .

After the seizure of Czechoslovakia fascist Germany proceeded with her preparations for war quite openly, before the eyes of the whole world. Hitler, encouraged by Britain and France, no longer stood on ceremony or pretended to favor the peaceful settlement of European problems. The most dramatic months of the prewar period had come. At that time it was already clear that every day was bringing mankind nearer to the unparalleled catastrophe of war.

What was, at that time, the policy of the Soviet Union on the one hand, and of Great Britain and France on the other?

The attempt of the falsifiers of history in the United States of America to avoid answering this question merely goes to prove that their consciences are not clear.

The truth is that even during the fatal period of the spring and summer of 1939, on the threshold of war, Britain and France, supported by ruling circles in the United States, continued the former course of their policy. This was a policy of provocative incitement of Hitler Germany against the Soviet Union, camouflaged not only with pharisaical phrases about their readiness to cooperate with the Soviet Union, but also with certain simple diplomatic maneuvers intended to conceal the real character of their policy from world public opinion.

Among such maneuvers were, in the first place, the 1939 negotiations which Britain and France decided to open with the Soviet Union. In order to deceive public opinion, the ruling circles in Britain and France tried to depict these negotiations as a serious attempt to prevent the further extension of Hitlerite aggression. In the light of all the subsequent developments, however, it became perfectly clear that so far as the Anglo-French side was concerned, these negotiations were from the very beginning nothing but another move in their double game. . . .

The negotiations between Britain and France on the one hand, and the Soviet

Union on the other, began in March, 1939, and continued for about four months.

The whole course of these negotiations showed with perfect clarity that whereas the Soviet Union was trying to reach a broad agreement with the Western Powers on the basis of equality, an agreement capable of preventing Germany, even though at the last moment, from starting a war in Europe, the Governments of Britain and France, relying on support in the United States, set themselves entirely different aims. The ruling circles in Britain and France, accustomed to having others pull their chestnuts out of the fire, on this occasion too attempted to foist obligations upon the Soviet Union under which the USSR would have taken upon itself the brunt of the sacrifice in repulsing a possible Hitler aggression, while Britain and France would not bind themselves by any commitment to the Soviet Union.

If the rulers of Britain and France had succeeded in this maneuver they would have come much closer to attaining their basic aim, which was to get Germany and the Soviet Union to come to grips as quickly as possible. The Soviet Government, however, saw through this scheme, and at all stages in the negotiations it countered the diplomatic trickery and subterfuges of the Western Powers with its clear and frank proposals intended to serve but one purpose — the safeguarding of peace in Europe.

There is no need to recall all the vicissitudes through which the negotiations went. We need only bring to mind a few of the more important points. It suffices to recall the terms put forward during the negotiations by the Soviet Government: the conclusion of an effective pact of mutual assistance against aggression between Britain, France, and the USSR; the granting of a guarantee by Britain, France, and the USSR to states of Central and Eastern Europe, including all the European countries bordering on the USSR, without exception; the conclusion of a concrete military agreement between Britain, France,

and the USSR on the forms and volume of immediate effective aid to each other and to the guaranteed states in the event of an attack by aggressors.

At the Third Session of the Supreme Soviet of the USSR on May 31, 1939, V. M. Molotov pointed out that some of the Anglo-French proposals moved during those negotiations had contained none of the elementary principles of reciprocity and equality of obligations, indispensable for all agreements between equals.

"While guaranteeing themselves," said V. M. Molotov, "from direct attack on the part of aggressors by mutual assistance pacts between themselves and with Poland and while trying to secure for themselves the assistance of the USSR in the event of an attack by aggressors on Poland and Romania, the British and French left open the question of whether the USSR in its turn might count on their assistance in the event of its being directly attacked by aggressors, just as they left open another question, namely, whether they could participate in guaranteeing the small states bordering on the USSR and covering its northwestern frontier, should these states prove unable to defend their neutrality from attack by aggressors. Thus, the position was one of inequality for the USSR."

Even when the British and French representatives gave verbal consent to the principle of mutual assistance on terms of reciprocity between Britain, France, and the USSR in the event of a direct attack by an aggressor, they hedged it in with a number of reservations which rendered this consent fictitious.

In addition to this, the Anglo-French proposals provided for help on the part of the USSR to those countries to which the British and French had given promises of guarantees, but they said nothing about their own help for the countries on the northwestern frontier of the USSR, the Baltic States, in the event of an aggressor attacking them.

In view of the above-mentioned considerations, V. M. Molotov announced that the

Soviet Union could not undertake obligations with respect to some countries unless similar guarantees were given with respect to the countries situated on the northwestern frontier of the Soviet Union. . . .

A circumstance that attracted attention at the time was that men of secondary importance were sent to conduct the negotiations on behalf of Great Britain in Moscow, while Chamberlain himself went to Germany to carry on negotiations with Hitler, and that on several occasions. It is also important to note that the British representative for the negotiations with the USSR, Strang, had no authority to sign any agreement with the Soviet Union.

In view of the demand of the Soviet Union that the parties should proceed to concrete negotiations concerning measures to fight a possible aggressor, the Governments of Britain and France had to consent to send their military missions to Moscow. But it took those missions an unusually long time to get to Moscow, and when they did get there, it transpired that they were composed of men of secondary importance who, furthermore, had not been authorized to sign any agreement. That being the case, the military negotiations proved to be as futile as the political ones.

The military missions of the Western Powers demonstrated at once that they even had no desire to carry on serious conversations concerning means of mutual assistance in the event of aggression on the part of Germany. The Soviet military mission proceeded from the fact that, since the USSR had no common border with Germany, it could render Britain, France, and Poland assistance in the event of war only if Soviet troops were permitted to pass through Polish territory. The Polish Government, however, declared that it would accept no military assistance from the Soviet Union, thus showing that it feared the growth of strength of the Soviet Union more than Hitler's aggression. Both the British and French missions supported Poland's position.

In the course of the military negotiations, the question also came up as to the strength of the armed forces which should be put in the field at once by the parties to the agreement in the event of aggression. The British named a ridiculous figure, stating that they could put in the field five infantry divisions and one mechanized division. That was what the British offered at a time when the Soviet Union declared that it was prepared to send to the front against the aggressor one hundred and thirty-six divisions, five thousand medium and heavy guns, up to ten thousand tanks and whippets, more than five thousand war planes, etc. The above shows with what an utter lack of seriousness the British Government treated the negotiations for a military agreement with the USSR.

The facts cited above fully bear out the conclusion that suggests itself, and this conclusion is as follows:

(1) Throughout the negotiations the Soviet Government strove with the utmost patience to secure agreement with Britain and France for mutual assistance against an aggressor on a basis of equality and on the condition that the mutual assistance would be really effective, i.e., that the signing of a political agreement would be accompanied by the signing of a military convention establishing the volume, forms, and time limits of the assistance, as all the preceding events had shown clearly enough that only such an agreement could be effective and might bring the Hitlerite aggressor to his senses, encouraged though he was by complete impunity and by the connivance of the Western Powers during the course of many years.

(2) Britain's and France's behavior during the negotiations with the Soviet Union fully confirmed that a serious agreement was farthest from their thoughts, since British and French policy was guided by other aims which had nothing in common with the interests of peace and the fight against aggression.

(3) The perfidious purpose of Anglo-French policy was to give Hitler to understand that the USSR had no allies, that the

USSR was isolated, that he could attack the USSR without running the risk of encountering the resistance of Britain and France.

It was no wonder, therefore, that Anglo-French-Soviet negotiations ended in failure.

There was, of course, nothing fortuitous about that failure. It was becoming ever more obvious that the breakdown of the negotiations had been planned beforehand by the representatives of the Western Powers in their double game. The point was that, along with open negotiation with the USSR, *the British conducted backstage negotiations with Germany, and they attached incomparably greater importance to the latter*. . . .

By this time there was already no doubt left that, far from intending to make any serious attempt to prevent Hitler Germany from starting the war, Britain and France, on the contrary, were doing everything within their power, by means of secret deals and agreements, by means of every possible kind of provocation, to incite Hitler Germany against the Soviet Union.

No forgers will ever succeed in wiping from history or from the consciousness of the peoples the decisive fact that under these conditions, the Soviet Union faced the alternative: either to accept, for purposes of self defense, Germany's proposal to conclude a non-aggression pact and thereby to ensure to the Soviet Union the prolongation of peace for a certain period of time, which might be used by the Soviet State better to prepare its forces for resistance to a possible attack on the part of an aggressor; or to reject Germany's proposal for a non-aggression pact and thereby to permit war provocateurs from the camp of the Western Powers immediately to involve the Soviet Union in armed conflict with Germany at a time when the situation was utterly unfavorable to the Soviet Union and when it was completely isolated.

In this situation, the Soviet Government found itself compelled to make its choice and conclude a non-aggression pact with Germany.

This choice was a wise and far-sighted act of Soviet foreign policy under the conditions which then obtained. This step of the Soviet Government to an enormous extent predetermined the favorable outcome of the Second World War for the Soviet Union and for all the freedom-loving peoples.

It would be a gross slander to assert that the conclusion of a pact with the Hitlerites was part of the plan of the foreign policy of the USSR. On the contrary, the USSR strove at all times to have an agreement with the Western non-aggressive states against the German and Italian aggressors for the achievement of collective security on the basis of equality. But there must be two parties to an agreement.

Whereas the USSR insisted on an agreement for combating aggression, Britain and France systematically rejected it, preferring to pursue a policy of isolating the USSR, a policy of concessions to the aggressors, a policy of directing aggression to the East, against the USSR.

The United States of America, far from counteracting that ruinous policy, backed it in every way. As for the American billionaires, they went on investing their capital in German heavy industries, helping the Germans to expand their war industries, and thus supplying German aggression with arms. They might as well be saying: "Go on, Messrs. Europeans, wage war to your hearts' content; wage war with God's help; while we, modest American billionaires, will accumulate wealth out of your war, making hundreds of millions of dollars in super-profits."

Naturally, with this state of affairs in Europe, there only remained one way out for the Soviet Union: to accept the German proposal for a pact. This was, after all, the best of all the possible ways out. . . .

ROOSEVELT REBUKED

CHARLES CALLAN TANSILL

Before 1952, Charles Callan Tansill was best known as author of a study of American involvement in the First World War, *America Goes to War* (1938). Like other "isolationists" of the 1930's Tansill insisted that President Woodrow Wilson needlessly led the United States into war in 1917. In *Back Door to War* (1952), Tansill—professor of history at Georgetown University—pressed a similar interpretation: that President Franklin D. Roosevelt, determined to take the United States into the war against Germany in Europe, used events in the Pacific (the "Back Door to War" in Europe) in order to shake the American people out of their contentment with neutrality. Tansill also argued that Roosevelt, deliberately and without provocation by Hitler, was hostile toward Nazi Germany from 1933 until 1939; when war came, Roosevelt's policy had helped to cause it. This reading gives the essence of Tansill's argument: that Roosevelt stiffened the resistance of the British, French, and Poles against Hitler's demands in 1939. The argument is in diametrical opposition to the Soviet contention that the United States encouraged Hitler's Germany in aggression against the Soviet Union. But Tansill's interpretation has one thing in common with the Soviet view: both present scathing condemnations of American policy in the diplomacy of the 1930's.

I n London, Lord Halifax [early in September, 1939] confided to Ambassador Kennedy that the outbreak of war reminded him of a dream he once had in which he was being tried for murder. When he was finally convicted and found guilty he was surprised what a feeling of relief came over him. It was very much the same now; he had planned in all ways to keep away a World War and had worked himself into a sad state of health and now that he had failed he found himself freshened up for the new struggle. . . .

It became more and more apparent to one as Halifax talked . . . that what Britain depends on more than anything else to end the war before the world collapses, is the internal collapse inside of Germany. They had definite confidence in their secret service reports that the oil and gasoline supply is definitely not over four months and that there is a definite feeling in Germany against war and if it got too tough economically, Hitler would be out.

The reports of British intelligence experts were as inaccurate in military matters as they were with reference to gas and oil supplies in the Reich. General Ironside informed the British Cabinet, on the basis of a series of reports, that German strategy was based upon a quick campaign. Some of the terrain leading into Polish territory was quite rugged. If the Poles made it "tough" for the invading Germans "so that it required a couple of months to make any headway," Hitler's "hordes would have great difficulty in retreating or advancing."

The American military attaché in Berlin was equally optimistic with regard to checking the progress of the German mili-

From Charles Callan Tansill, *Back Door to War: The Roosevelt Foreign Policy, 1933–1941* (Chicago, 1952), pp. 554–557. Reprinted by permission of Henry Regnery Company.

tary machine. The Poles were following a preconceived plan that envisaged "delaying the German advance with covering forces and stubbornly holding fortified areas. . . . They are making the Germans pay dearly for every kilometer gained and are exhausting the best German divisions." The Polish defense was "being carried out as planned by the Poles and the French and British missions, and appears to be succeeding."

These dispatches from Berlin read like chapters from *Alice in Wonderland,* and in 1939 it appeared as though Neville Chamberlain was assuming the role of the Mad Hatter when he could not send even token assistance to the hard-pressed Poles. Nowadays it seems evident that the real Mad Hatter was Franklin D. Roosevelt who pressed Chamberlain to give promises to the Poles when there was no possibility of fulfilling them. According to some reports, it was William C. Bullitt who cast Roosevelt in this grotesque role.

I recently received from Mr. Verne Marshall, former editor of the *Cedar Rapids Gazette,* a letter in which he made the following significant statements:

President Roosevelt wrote a note to William Bullitt [in the summer of 1939], then Ambassador to France, directing him to advise the French Government that if, in the event of a Nazi attack upon Poland, France and England did not go to Poland's aid, those countries could expect no help from America if a general war developed. On the other hand, if France and England immediately declared war on Germany [in the event of a Nazi attack upon Poland], they could expect "all aid" from the United States.

F.D.R.'s instructions to Bullitt were to send this word along to "Joe" and "Tony," meaning Ambassadors Kennedy, in London, and Biddle, in Warsaw, respectively. F.D.R. wanted Daladier, Chamberlain and Josef Beck to know of these instructions to Bullitt. Bullitt merely sent his note from F.D.R. to Kennedy in the diplomatic pouch from Paris. Kennedy followed Bullitt's idea and forwarded it to Biddle. When the Nazis grabbed Warsaw and Beck disappeared, they must have come

into possession of the F.D.R. note. The man who wrote the report I sent you, saw it in Berlin in October, 1939.

After receiving this letter from Mr. Marshall I wrote at once to Mr. Bullitt and inquired about this alleged instruction from the President. He replied as follows: "I have no memory of any instruction from President Roosevelt of the nature quoted in your letter to me and feel quite certain that no such instruction was ever sent to me by the President."

Mr. Joseph Kennedy sent to me a similar negative answer with reference to this alleged instruction from the President, but the *Forrestal Diaries* would indicate that Bullitt did strongly urge President Roosevelt to exert pressure upon Prime Minister Chamberlain and that Roosevelt responded to this pressure. The following excerpt has far-reaching implications:

27 December 1945: Played golf today with Joe Kennedy [Joseph P. Kennedy, who was Roosevelt's Ambassador to Great Britain in the years immediately before the war]. I asked him about his conversations with Roosevelt and Neville Chamberlain from 1938 on. He said Chamberlain's position in 1938 was that England had nothing with which to fight and that she could not risk going to war with Hitler. Kennedy's view: That Hitler would have fought Russia without any later conflict with England if it had not been for Bullitt's [William C. Bullitt, then Ambassador to France] urging on Roosevelt in the summer of 1939 that the Germans must be faced down about Poland; neither the French nor the British would have made Poland a cause of war if it had not been for the constant needling from Washington. Bullitt, he said, kept telling Roosevelt that the Germans wouldn't fight; Kennedy that they would, and that they would overrun Europe. Chamberlain, he says, stated that America and the world Jews had forced England into the war. In his telephone conversations with Roosevelt in the summer of 1939 the President kept telling him to put some iron up Chamberlain's backside. Kennedy's response always was that putting iron up his backside did no good unless the British

had some iron with which to fight, and they did not. . . .

What Kennedy told me in this conversation jibes substantially with the remarks Clarence Dillon had made to me already, to the general effect that Roosevelt had asked him in some manner to communicate privately with the British to the end that Chamberlain should have greater firmness in his dealings with Germany. Dillon told me that at Roosevelt's request he had talked with Lord Lothian in the same general sense as Kennedy reported Roosevelt having urged him to do with Chamberlain. Lothian presumably was to communicate to Chamberlain the gist of his conversation with Dillon.

Looking backward there is undoubtedly foundation for Kennedy's belief that Hitler's attack could have been deflected to Russia.

Mr. Kennedy is known to have a good memory and it is highly improbable that his statements to Secretary Forrestal were entirely untrustworthy. Ambassador Bullitt was doing a lot of talking in 1939 and he was regarded as the mouthpiece of the President. In January 1939 he had a long conversation with Count Jerzy Potocki, the Polish Ambassador in Washington, and left him with the impression that "he [Bullitt] had received from President Roosevelt a very detailed definition of the attitude taken by the United States towards the present European crisis. He will present this material at the Quai d'Orsay. . . . The contents of these directions . . . were: (1) The vitalizing foreign policy, under the leadership of President Roosevelt, severely and unambiguously condemns totalitarian countries; . . . (2) it is the decided opinion of the President that France and Britain must put [an] end to any sort of compromise with the totalitarian countries."

In February 1939, Bullitt had a conversation with Jules Lukasiewicz, the Polish Ambassador in Paris, and once again he seemed to speak with authority. He confided to Lukasiewicz that Washington official circles were greatly concerned about the outbreak of war in Europe. If Britain and France were defeated, Germany "would become dangerous to the realistic interests of the United States on the American continent. For this reason, one can foresee right from the beginning the participation of the United States in the war on the side of France and Britain. . . . One thing . . . seems certain to me, namely, that the policy of President Roosevelt will henceforth take the course of supporting France's resistance . . . and to weaken British compromise tendencies."

These excerpts from the dispatches of the Polish ambassadors in Washington and in Paris afford a clear indication of the fact that President Roosevelt, through Bullitt, was exerting steady pressure upon Britain and France to stand up boldly to Nazi Germany. When this policy led to a war in which Nazi armed forces easily crushed French resistance, it is easy now to understand the poignancy of Premier Reynaud's pleas to Roosevelt for prompt assistance. He and Daladier had taken the assurances of Bullitt seriously and the hysterical tone of Reynaud's repeated wires to the White House indicates a feeling of betrayal. From the battered walls of Warsaw there were loud murmurs about broken British promises. When their muted echoes reached London, Neville Chamberlain must have remembered the constant "needling from Washington" in favor of a more resolute stand against Hitler, and Joseph Kennedy must have had reluctant recollections of the many occasions when the President "kept telling him to put some iron up Chamberlain's backside." Germany had been baited into a war with Britain and France when she would have preferred a conflict with Russia over the Ukraine. Chamberlain got plenty of iron up his backside, but it was Nazi hot metal that seared him and all Britain and helped to break into bits a proud empire that all the King's horses and all the King's men can never put together again.

POLISH BLUNDER?

HENRY L. ROBERTS

Probably the most valuable single book treating European diplomacy between the two World Wars is a large collection of essays edited by Gordon A. Craig and Felix Gilbert, _The Diplomats, 1919–1939_ (1953). This reading is taken from an essay in that volume treating the policies of Colonel Józef Beck, Minister of Foreign Affairs in Poland's authoritarian government from 1932 until the defeat of 1939. The author of this essay, Henry L. Roberts, is a specialist in the history of Central-Eastern Europe and Director of The Russian Institute at Columbia University. This reading provides some support for the thesis that Poland must share responsibility for the outbreak of the Second World War, though Roberts is more interested in explaining Polish policy than condemning it. His explanation is highly relevant to the discussion in previous readings of responsibility for the failure of the U.S.S.R. and the West to achieve a common front against Nazi Germany in 1939. It is also relevant to Hitler's contention early in 1939 that he wanted to cooperate with Poland rather than to destroy it.

AMONG the public figures of countries overrun by Nazi Germany, Colonel Józef Beck, Poland's Foreign Minister from 1932 to 1939, has probably received the least sympathy. Despite his determined resistance to Hitler's threats in the crisis leading to the outbreak of the second world war, he has been remembered as one of the Pilsudskian _epigoni_, as the man who refused to work with the Little Entente or the League of Nations, who pursued, in substance, a pro-German policy after 1934, who joined in the dismembering of Czechoslovakia, and, finally, as the man whose stubborn refusal to enter any combination with the Russians contributed to the failure of the Anglo-French-Soviet negotiations of the spring and summer of 1939.

After Poland's defeat and Beck's internment in Rumania the world heard little of him. He died in obscurity, of tuberculosis, on June 5, 1944. Less than a year after his death the war of which his country was first victim came to an end, but Poland soon fell under the domination of the Power that Beck always felt to be the ultimate enemy. This retrospective vindication of his Russian policy, the postwar publication of Polish, French, German, and British evidence bearing on his activities, and the recent appearance of Beck's own diplomatic memoirs suggest a reappraisal of this controversial and rather elusive figure. . . .

In the spring and summer of 1933, Hitler, publicly and privately, gave reassurances to the Poles that he had no intention of violating existing treaties or stirring up trouble in Danzig. In November, the Polish government explained to Hitler that Poland's security was founded on direct relations with other states and on collaboration through the League of Nations. Since Germany had now withdrawn from the League, the Polish government wished to know whether there was any chance "of

From Henry L. Roberts, "The Diplomacy of Colonel Beck," in Gordon A. Craig and Felix Gilbert (eds.), _The Diplomats, 1919–1939_ (Princeton, 1953), pp. 579, 601–611. Reprinted by permission of Princeton University Press and Oxford University Press.

compensating for the loss of this element of security, in direct Polish-German relations." From this opening, the path led directly to the signing of the nonaggression agreement of January 26, 1934; and there is no indication in Beck's memoirs that, after getting a favorable German response, Pilsudski turned once more to France before signing the agreement.

Without doubt, Beck himself was much pleased with the German pact, which he regarded as the greatest and most valuable achievement of Polish foreign policy. After Pilsudski's death, he paid a cordial visit to Berlin and was able to reassure the Nazi leaders that Polish policy would not change with the Marshal's passing. Commenting on that visit, he wrote later: "It will doubtless be very interesting one day to study to what degree the complete reversal of German policy several years later can or should be attributed to Hitler himself, in what measure eventually it was owing to the overly great ease with which his imperialist policy went from success to success, or, finally, if and to what point it had its origin in a reaction of the old Prussian spirit in the interior of Germany itself."

Here seems to be the real clue to Beck's policy vis-à-vis Germany. While no pro-German, he was definitely attracted by, and had confidence in, what he thought to be the Hitlerian foreign policy. He had no illusions that it was a static policy, but he thought it was based on nationalist principles. Consequently, he expected an attempt to take over Austria and, subsequently, action against Czechoslovakia; but he was quite willing to accept these developments as not imperiling Poland.

Beck never felt that he was becoming a German satellite or compromising the independence of Poland's foreign policy. He did not join Germany in an anti-Bolshevik or anti-Russian crusade, although he was gratified whenever the Nazis told him of their dislike, not merely of Communism, but of any Russian state whatever its complexion. As early as the autumn of 1934, Göring had thrown out some hints that

Poland might well join Germany in an anti-Russian agreement, but Pilsudski "cut short this conversation by declaring that Poland, a country bordering Russia, had to adopt toward that Power a moderate and calm policy and could not adhere to any combination of the sort to revive tension on our eastern frontiers." Beck appears to have held to this view in face of subsequent hints and offers.

Some authors, Polish and of other nationalities, have gone so far as to argue that the chief fault of Beck's diplomacy was not the German connection, which was actually Pilsudski's responsibility, but the fact that, having achieved it, he did not then ride it for all it was worth. It is difficult to guess how such a venture might have turned out. In the short run, gains in the east might have compensated for the loss of Danzig and control over the Corridor. But, at the end of this road lay Machiavelli's warning: "A prince ought to take care never to make an alliance with one more powerful than himself for the purpose of attacking others, unless necessity compels him . . . because if he conquers, you are at his discretion."

Even Beck's unpleasant performance at the time of the Munich crisis was not planned in concert with the Germans. Western diplomats as well as many Poles felt, in the summer of 1938, that Poland's rapprochement with Germany was "degenerating into an undignified imitation of the small fish that seek their meat in the wake of the shark." Nevertheless, Beck insisted he was pursuing an independent policy. As he later expressed it, "I formulated on the part of Poland a simple and at the same time very supple demand. I declared we demanded simply that, if the government of Prague decided to make concessions to other countries, our interests should be treated in exactly the same fashion. When the diplomats asked me to define our demands or claims, I categorically refused to do so and affirmed that Poland did not have the intention of dismembering the Czechoslovak state or of taking the initiative in an attack against this country, and that, consequently, it did not feel called upon to give a rigid precision to its claims. That if, however, the Czechoslovak state, a veritable mosaic of nationalities hitherto governed by methods of brutal centralisation, had the intention of revising its policy or its regime in order to take better account of the interests of a particular national group, we could not admit that the Polish minority, which was grouped in a very compact manner in a region situated on our frontier, should be less well treated than any other ethnic group."

Having taken this "most favored nation" attitude, Beck was bound to be evasive when queried by the French or British ambassadors. The Germans, however, were equally uncertain of his intentions. On July 1, the German ambassador, Moltke, reported on a conversation with Beck: "As usual, when he wishes to avoid definite statements, M. Beck said a great deal without saying anything of importance." Moltke doubted that Poland would side with France if it intervened, but he would not assume that Poland would be on Germany's side. "Poland will . . . always act exclusively according to her own interests." In September, Moltke denied rumors that he had been trying to influence Poland. "Practical cooperation already exists and great emphasis on this point would not be advisable in view of M. Beck's disposition. . . . It is correct to say that Beck attached great importance to achieving Polish aims as far as possible independently and that he is trying particularly to avoid giving the outside world any impression of dependence on Germany."

The basic danger in Beck's "supple" policy was that the more Germany raised its claims, the more he was obliged to raise his. As the dispute moved beyond autonomy for the Sudeten Germans to the right of self-determination and plebiscites, Beck came to demand equivalent treatment for the Polish minority. When the decision was reached to cede certain Sudeten territories without a plebiscite, the Poles in turn demanded frontier revision without plebiscite. By September 21, the Polish government was pressing hard on the Czechs, denouncing the 1925 Polish-Czech convention dealing with minorities and demanding rapid action. To the Czech appeal for negotiation, the Poles responded even more peremptorily, in part because of a belief that the Soviet note of September 23, threatening to cancel the Polish-Soviet non-aggression pact, was somehow related to the Czech notes.

Then came the Munich Conference at which the dispute was suddenly taken over by that old enemy of Polish diplomacy, the Four Powers. Germany gained its demands; Poland was not even invited to the meeting. Beck decided that an immediate reaction was in order and asked for a march on Teschen as a "protest against the Munich proceedings." On September 30, he sent a twelve-hour ultimatum to the Czechs, the text of which, as Beneš subsequently remarked, was "almost identical with the ultimatum which Hitler sent to Beck himself a year later with respect to the solution of the question of Danzig." This was not Colonel Beck's finest hour.

The first inkling that Polish-German relations were up for review came shortly after Munich when, on October 24, Ribbentrop proposed to the Polish ambassador a general settlement of issues between Poland and Germany. This settlement included the reunion of Danzig with the Reich, an extraterritorial road and railway across Pomorze, a guarantee of frontiers, joint action in colonial matters, and a common policy toward Russia on the basis of the Anti-Comintern Pact. Beck's response was conciliatory but held that "any attempt to incorporate the Free City into the Reich must inevitably lead to conflict."

According to Beck, writing in October 1939, the turning point in his own mind concerning relations with Germany was his interview with Hitler on January 4 of that year. To his alarm he noted "new accents" in Hitler's remarks. The Chancellor, while continuing to propose German-Polish cooperation, now "treated with levity the ideas which he and German propaganda had hitherto elevated almost to the level of a religion." Still unwilling to revise his estimate of Hitler, Beck thought that perhaps the Fuehrer was still inclined to be cautious but that Ribbentrop, "a dangerous personality," was urging a reckless course. Upon his return to Warsaw, Beck felt sufficiently alarmed to tell Moscicki and Smigly-Rydz that these shifts in the German mood might presage war. Ribbentrop visited Warsaw later in the month, but the conversations were not fruitful. Beck refused to give way on Danzig or Pomorze despite suggested compensation in Slovakia and even mention of the Black Sea.

With the German occupation of Prague and Memel in March, the situation deteriorated rapidly. If Poland's Ukrainian problem had been relieved by Hungary's taking over Ruthenia, this gain was far outweighed by Germany's annexation of Bohemia and Moravia and its virtual military control over Slovakia, which, as General Jodl said, now made it possible to "consider the Polish problem on the basis of more or less favorable strategic premises." By March 28 the German ambassador was accusing Beck of wanting "to negotiate at the point of a bayonet." To which Beck replied, "That is your own method."

Thus, Beck's efforts to maintain good yet independent relations with Germany had come to failure. His basic error was a misreading of the Nazi movement and of Hitler's personality. That he was deeply chagrined by this turn of events, which undid his whole diplomatic strategy, is not surprising. It was reported that, after his highly popular speech of May 5, in which he courageously stood up against the German menaces, "in a fit of rage, [he] had thrown a whole pile of congratulatory telegrams into a corner."

Whatever Beck's personal feelings, it was clear that if he was to resist Germany he had to look abroad. Britain, and secondarily France, were the Powers to which he necessarily turned. But, as has been observed above, by the spring of 1939 it was far from certain that Britain and France were capable of rescuing Poland. Polish-Soviet relations now assumed decisive importance.

Although Pilsudski and Beck declared that their policy was to keep Poland evenly balanced between Germany and the Soviet Union, Polish diplomacy was in practice perceptibly off-center. Pilsudski brought with him the deep anti-Russian feelings of his revolutionary and wartime career. To these were added a justifiable suspicion of Bolshevik intentions and a concern about the large Ukrainian and White Russian minorities in Poland's eastern provinces. As in many states bordering on Russia, the outcome was a conviction on the part of the government, so pervasive as to be almost unspoken and undebated, that no positive and fruitful relationship with the Soviet Union was possible. In the 1920's, a Polish ambassador returning from Moscow reported to Pilsudski that he had not tried to settle conflicts of little importance but had rather sought to ameliorate general relations between the two countries. The Marshal interrupted him to say, "Now, that is curious. I should have done exactly the opposite." While Beck always stressed the importance of an independent Polish policy and the value of bilateral negotiations, he was not enthusiastic about dealing bilaterally with the Soviet Union. When discussing in his memoirs the negotiations leading to the Polish-Soviet pact of 1932, he observed that Poland's traditional policy demanded "solidarity with all the western neighbors of Russia." There was no equivalent sense of a need for solidarity with Germany's eastern neighbors when it came to negotiating with that Power.

Certain steps were taken, however. Poland (along with Estonia, Latvia, and Rumania) signed the Litvinov protocol on February 9, 1929, the Polish-Soviet pact of nonaggression of July 25, 1932, and — with Russia's other neighbors — the London convention for the definition of aggression of

July 3, 1933; and, in 1934, Beck made his trip to Moscow to balance the signing of the German-Polish pact.

Within the next two years, however, Polish-Soviet relations fell off greatly. In July 1936 the new Polish ambassador in Moscow, Grzybowski, was received by Krestinsky, Litvinov's deputy, with blunt words: "The political relations between us could not be worse. We are working to increase the prestige of the League of Nations, and for collective security; we are combatting all forms of aggression and all forms of fascism. At the present time we are pursuing an anti-German, anti-Italian and anti-Japanese policy. Poland is pursuing a diametrically contrary policy, tending to weaken the League of Nations, combatting attempts to realize collective security, supporting Italy and sympathizing with Japan. Poland is within the orbit of German policy."

Grzybowski, of course, denied this interpretation and his rather rueful comment on this meeting must sound familiar to those who have had occasion to deal with the Soviet Union: "Irrespective of Polish policy, the Soviets constantly interpreted it so as to contrapose it to their own policy." Nevertheless, it is true that Beck disapproved of the Soviet entry into the League of Nations, regarded collective security as a Communist device, and was highly critical of France and Czechoslovakia for signing treaties of mutual assistance with the USSR. Indeed, the more one considers the course of Polish diplomacy the more this deep-rooted and altogether natural mistrust of Russia seems to give a distinct flavor to Polish attitudes on almost all issues. Beck said at the end of his career, "In the course of the twenty years of my political activity in the field of foreign affairs, I acquired the conviction that the essential element which created divergences between Polish policy and French policy was not the German question but, invariably, the manner of viewing the Russian problem."

Beck not only regarded the Soviet Union as a dangerous power but he denied that it could serve as a counterweight to Germany, notwithstanding the mutual hostility of these two powers in the 1930's. In 1937 he and Winston Churchill informally discussed this issue while relaxing at Cannes but were unable to agree. "I could not avoid the impression," Beck later wrote, "that this eminent statesman lived too much on his memories of the preceding war and that he was too inclined to consider Russia as a relatively important counterweight to German dynamism. I tried to make him understand that Europe could not have the least confidence in Soviet Russia and that we, its neighbors, had more evidence than anyone for judging the Russian phenomenon with skepticism."

When Beck went to London in April 1939 to negotiate the British-Polish mutual assistance pact, he felt he should state Poland's position on having Russia as an alliance partner. Poland, he said, had no confidence in Russia or in the ends it pursued. It had had experience with Tsarist imperialism and with Communist imperialism, and they came to the same thing. However, in face of the German menace, there was no point in rebuffing Russia; one should at least be assured of its neutrality. Though doubtful of its achievement, he would not oppose an English-French-Soviet entente, but such an accord could not impose new obligations on Poland. He would be satisfied if an arrangement were made whereby, in case of war with Germany, arms could be sent to Poland via Russia and Russia could provide raw materials.

The involved story of the unsuccessful efforts by the British and French to reconcile this position with the mounting demands of the Russians in the abortive negotiations of the spring and summer of 1939 cannot be told here. There is no question, however, that the Polish refusal to agree to the presence of Soviet troops on Polish soil was, as a debating point at least, an important factor in the breakdown of the negotiations. The reluctance of the Poles to make this concession is certainly understandable, nor is it by any means certain that a greater show of cooperation on their part would have deflected the Soviet Union from its pact of August 23 with Germany. Nevertheless, the utterly negative quality of Polish-Soviet relations appears very clearly in a set of conditions laid down by the Polish ambassador in a conversation with Molotov in May 1939: "We could not accept a one-sided Soviet guarantee. Nor could we accept a mutual guarantee, because in the event of a conflict with Germany our forces would be completely engaged, and so we would not be in any position to give help to the Soviets. Also we could not accept collective negotiations, and made our adoption of a definite attitude conditional on the result of the Anglo-Franco-Soviet negotiations. We rejected all discussion of matters affecting us other than by the bilateral method. . . . I indicated our favorable attitude to the Anglo-Franco-Soviet negotiations, and once more emphasized our entire loyalty in relation to the Soviets. In the event of conflict we by no means rejected specified forms of Soviet aid, but considered it premature to determine them definitely. We considered it premature to open bilateral negotiations with the Soviets before the Anglo-Franco-Soviet negotiations had achieved a result." The ambassador continued, "M. Molotov made no objection whatever." Indeed, there seemed to be very little to say.

Interestingly enough, Beck was quite pleased that Molotov had replaced Litvinov, whom he regarded as the "notorious enemy of our country." "It was possible to suppose that the anti-Polish complex peculiar to this man, who was by origin a *litwak,* had disappeared with him."[1] Just as Hitler, an Austrian, was to alter the anti-Polish bias of the Prussian tradition, so, presumably, Molotov was to rid Soviet policy of the anti-Polish prejudices of the *litwak* Litvinov. Here again Beck's own nationalism was misleading him. By reducing foreign policy to such motives he was unable to grasp the

basic drives of either the Nazi or the Soviet dictatorship.

For a brief period, it is true, Molotov adopted toward the Poles an attitude of "the greatest courtesy." The Soviet government offered to supply them with war materials; the Soviet press urged resistance to German demands. In retrospect, of course, this amiability, which continued until the German attack, appears altogether sinister: intended at first to conceal the German-Soviet rapprochement and then, perhaps, to prolong Polish resistance in the event France and Great Britain failed to declare war on Germany.

In this instance, however, Beck's position did not change. To the last he refused to have Soviet troops on Polish territory; and the most he would concede was that, after hostilities had started, he might agree to reexamine the question with a view to possible Soviet-Polish cooperation.

Beck's diplomatic career ended in complete disaster. All his policies turned against him. The nonaggression pact with Hitler did not prevent a German assault; the disintegration of Czechoslovakia weakened rather then strengthened his southern frontier; his refusal to admit Russian soldiers to Polish soil did not keep them from overrunning eastern Poland in September 1939. Nor was this just bad luck. His views on the art of diplomacy, his estimate of the international situation, and his analysis of political motives were filled with inconsistencies that inevitably led to self-defeating policies.

He was not just an opportunist, though the charge of unprincipled opportunism has been laid against him. He adhered, rather arrogantly and purblindly, to a set of axioms which he took to be Pilsudskian heritage and which made up in their obvious preoccupation with the Polish national interest what they lacked in coherence and universality. But, unlike Churchill, who was fighting against the current and whose speeches of the 1930's have the real mark of prophetic insight, Beck was engulfed in

---

[1] Beck described the *litwak* as the "worst of the Jewish types."

the currents of his time, and his prophecies tended to be self-fulfilling ones which his own activities and outlook helped bring to pass.

Still, when all this has been said, an appraisal of Beck cannot be wholly negative. For all the errors of his policy, he was not one of the really malignant creatures of the decade. Contrary to widespread contemporary belief, he was not in league with Hitler, even though the two often appeared to be working in collaboration. Even in the case of his least defensible action, the ultimatum to Czechoslovakia, he was, to a large degree, the victim of his own "most favored nation" formula; the movement of events which drove him to such an unfortunate action came from the interaction of German aggressiveness and the wobbling retreat of the Western Powers, France and Great Britain. He did not like Czechoslovakia, but he did not plot its destruction.

Nor can one say that he contributed greatly to the disaster that overtook Europe, except in the sense that his actions fed into a vicious circle which intensified and compounded the weaknesses of the existing international order. The League of Nations was indeed a weak reed, though attitudes such as Beck's helped make it so. Russia was indeed a dangerous and unpredictable Power, though Beck's policy toward Russia did nothing to make it less dangerous or unpredictable and seemed to provide a rationale for Soviet actions in 1939. In this respect, he is highly symptomatic of the 1930's. The feeling, so apparent in his memoirs, that there were no feasible alternatives, was characteristic of a general European mood which was creating, and being created by, the approaching catastrophe.

In one regard, however, Beck definitely deserves respect. When the final test came, he did not yield. In a desperate situation, partly of his own making, he took an unprovocative but courageous stand. The result, to be sure, was a horrible war, the outcome of which was not real peace and which had tragic consequences for Poland during and after the hostilities. . . .

FOR AND AGAINST ITALIAN RESPONSIBILITY

L. B. NAMIER

The British historian Lewis B. Namier distinguished himself well before the outbreak of World War II by intensive and original studies of British politics in the eighteenth century. After 1945 his research and his crisp style were brought to bear on the causes of the Second World War. In articles and in three books he offered critical analyses of the events that led to war. This reading is representative of these works—which reviewed new memoirs, documents, and secondary studies—in that it is an essay on German-Italian relations, occasioned by the publication of a study of the subject by another noted historian, the Italian scholar Mario Toscano. Toscano made use of records left by Count Galeazzo Ciano, Mussolini's son-in-law and Foreign Minister, and documents from the archives of the Italian Foreign Ministry. Namier made the essence of this material available to English readers. Like Elizabeth Wiskemann, Namier shows how largely Mussolini had become by 1939 a satellite of Hitler. After reading this selection and others in this booklet you should be able to assess the degree to which Mussolini's Italy helped to encourage or prevent the outbreak of war in 1939.

THOUGH the Pact of Steel was a symptom rather than a factor in the history of 1939, the moves and methods of the Powers concerned are revealing; and the story of those negotiations is told with meticulous care and thorough knowledge by Professor Mario Toscano,[1] now Historical Adviser to the Italian Foreign Office and vice-president of the commission entrusted with the publication of the Italian diplomatic documents, 1861–1943. He has been able to supplement the material contained in Ciano's *Diary* and the published Ciano *Papers,* in the Nuremberg documents and those of the International Military Tribunal for the Far East, with unpublished Italian diplomatic telegrams and dispatches (among which those from Attolico, Ambassador in Berlin, are of outstanding interest), and with information derived from Italian survivors of those years. . . .

In May 1938, during Hitler's visit to Italy, Mussolini, who had just concluded an agreement with Great Britain and was negotiating one with France, thought of a pact which would give new contents to the Axis; or else people might start talking of its demise and of a return to Stresa. But the Italians were not prepared as yet to go the whole length of "a pact of military assistance, public or secret," as proposed by Ribbentrop. Ciano wrote in his *Diary* on May 6:

Ribbentrop . . . is exuberant and sometimes shows levity. The Duce says he is of the type of Germans that disgrace Germany. He talks right and left of war, without fixing either opponent or objective. Sometimes he wants, jointly with Japan, to destroy Russia. Or again his bolts strike France and England.

[1] Mario Toscano, *Le origini del patto d' acciaio.* Sansoni. Firenze. 1948.

From L. B. Namier, *Europe in Decay: A Study in Disintegration, 1936–1940* (London, 1950), pp. 129–144. Reprinted by courtesy of Macmillan & Co. Ltd., and by permission of Lady Namier.

Occasionally he threatens the United States. This puts me on my guard against his schemes.

When next, on June 19, Ribbentrop gave Attolico "confidentially" his "personal notions" on a German-Italian military alliance (the Führer "generally agrees with me in these matters"), he protested that Germany did not mean to drag Italy into a war over Czechoslovakia. The breach was widening between the democracies and the authoritarian States, and it was time for these to form a *bloc* and results were expected from the meeting of Hitler and Mussolini, "who are among the greatest personalities known to history." Attolico replied that Mussolini, in his recent speech at Genoa, had declared that in an ideological war "the totalitarian States would immediately form a *bloc*"; and, in accordance with instructions previously received, Attolico suggested the following points to be dealt with in an agreement: frontiers (the Alto Adige[2] and the removal of its German population); "consultation"; political and diplomatic support, possibly accompanied by secret military clauses. But, retorted Ribbentrop, why thus hide the element which has given the Axis its deterrent strength? What he wanted was "a plain, open military alliance" (*ipsissima verba*: Attolico did not speak German, and their talks were in English). Such an alliance alone would enable the two Powers to retain their gains and to realize their further aims. Italy would find them in the Mediterranean and Germany "for instance" in Czechoslovakia. He mentioned that he was sounding Tokyo about a "military triangle."

Ciano found Attolico's report "very important and interesting," and suggested a personal meeting (by now Mussolini was disappointed in Italy's agreement with Brittain, and was turning against one with France). In another talk at the end of July Attolico argued that the problems of the Danube Basin required clarification, as an object of discord it had replaced the

Anschluss in the calculations of their opponents. The next move occurred on September 30, at Munich, when Ribbentrop produced the draft of a tripartite German-Italian-Japanese alliance ("the greatest thing in the world"): it stipulated for consultation in diplomatic difficulties; political and diplomatic support should one of the contracting parties be threatened; and aid and assistance against unprovoked aggression. After signature the application of the treaty to particular cases was to be settled, and only when "the mode and extent of political, military, and economic assistance" were fixed would it come into force. (The political *éclat* would thus be secured, while heeding Japanese reluctance to assume ill-defined commitments.)

The precise nature of the Italian answer is not known (and probably it was not precise). Then, on October 23, Ribbentrop, having received a reply from the Japanese military and naval attachés, telephoned to Ciano: he was coming to Rome with a personal message from Hitler.

What does he want? [wrote Ciano in his *Diary*]. I mistrust Ribbentrop's initiatives. He is vain, frivolous, and loquacious. The Duce says that it is enough to look at his head to see that he lacks brains. Still more tact. I don't quite like the way those telephone calls of the last days were made. For the present we have to put up with it. But some time it will be necessary to call a halt to such making of policy by *coups de téléphone*.

Before Ribbentrop arrived in Rome, on October 27 Lord Perth informed Ciano that Britain was prepared to have the April agreement come into force as from the middle of November. "We must keep both doors open," noted Ciano in his *Diary*. "An alliance concluded now would close one of them, and not the less important, perhaps for ever." The same day the Japanese attachés communicated to him their counter-draft, which emphasized in its preamble the anti-Communist character of the treaty, but otherwise, with some minor additions, reproduced the three articles of

[2] Better known as the South Tyrol, which Austria was required in 1919 to cede to Italy.

the German draft. After a first talk with Ribbentrop Ciano wrote:

Ribbentrop has really come for a tripartite military alliance. . . . He has got into his head the idea of war, he wants war, his war . . . He does not name either enemies or objectives, but wants war in three or four years.

Ciano was more intelligent and subtle than Ribbentrop; yet the reader of his *Diary* feels that he judged the other man *en connaissance de cause;* though his critical sense did not extend to his own person.

The next day Ribbentrop expounded to Mussolini the Führer's reasons for wishing to see the triple military alliance concluded. War with the Western democracies was unavoidable within three or four years; and the present position of the Axis was "exceptionally favourable." Previously he had hesitated for fear of making England and France rearm, or causing the downfall of the appeasers, or provoking an Anglo-American alliance; now they were anyhow rearming as fast as they could, Chamberlain and Daladier were safe, and danger of war would render America merely more isolationist. Japan's power was formidable, but to refuse the pact might play into the hands of her pacifist "financiers."

The Czechoslovak crisis has proved our strength. We have the advantage of the initiative and are masters of the situation. We cannot be attacked. . . . Since September we can face war with the great democracies. . . . Czechoslovakia is practically finished. . . . Toward Poland the Reich means to pursue a policy of friendship respecting her vital needs, especially her access to the sea. . . . Russia is weak and will remain so for years to come: all our dynamic strength [*dinamismo*] can be directed against the democracies.

The Duce agreed that the alliance had to come, but doubted whether this was the time for it. An alliance was "a sacred pledge," to be observed in full. But while Italian public opinion accepted the Axis, it was not quite ripe for a military alliance.

When the time comes to conclude a German-Italian alliance, it will be necessary to fix objectives. We must not form a purely defensive alliance. There is no need for it, as no one thinks of attacking the totalitarian States. What we want is an alliance to redraw the map of the world. For this objectives and conquests will have to be fixed; we, for our part, know where we must go.

Mussolini envisaged a dual alliance only; whereas Japan entered into Hitler's *Weltpolitik* as a check on the United States and Russia, an alliance with her might have hindered rather than helped Mussolini at that juncture in his pursuit of Mediterranean objectives. Ribbentrop spoke of friendship with Poland: to Professor Toscano an example of Nazi "insincerity *erga omnes.*" While that insincerity can hardly be doubted, Ribbentrop's discourse exhibits one facet of Nazi policy at that juncture: the claims which he had raised against Poland in his talk with M. Lipski, Polish Ambassador in Berlin, on October 24 — and these were kept secret both from the Western Powers and from Italy — were not nearly as formidable as the offer he had made of German friendship. The formal inclusion in the Reich of an anyhow Nazified Danzig, and an extra-territorial *autostrade* across the Corridor, would not have cut off Poland's access to the sea, especially if she entered Germany's orbit; but her doing so would have severed her ties with the West and destroyed her independence. Although the direction suggested by Ribbentrop for Axis *dinamismo* followed that of Mussolini's interests, there was little response. Possibly Mussolini had learnt not to take Ribbentrop's schemes seriously; moreover, with all his braggadocio, he would not face a major war. Lastly an ephemeral personal factor influenced his attitude (a human proclivity unchecked in dictators):

At Munich [writes Professor Toscano] Mussolini, in appearance more than in reality (for his proposals had been supplied by the Germans) came out as arbitrator and mediator, though as one decidedly partial to the

Germans; who in the end aimed at obtaining even more. An alliance with Hitler, concluded so soon after, would obviously have made Mussolini lose the position he had acquired toward Britain and France, which he could not desire; nor could he wish to encourage new Nazi enterprises: he feared their bearing and repercussions on Italian interests, especially in the Danube Basin.

On November 23–24 Chamberlain and Lord Halifax visited Paris; meantime Germany was negotiating with France the Declaration of December 6. No great significance attached to either move (moreover, as appears from Ciano's *Diary,* the Germans had obtained a previous *nihil obstat* from Mussolini for their negotiations). None the less these developments grated on the Duce's excitable, unsteady disposition: on November 24 he telegraphed to Attolico that if the Anglo-French Entente was being transformed into "a true and proper military alliance," he would be prepared to conclude one with Germany immediately; and on the 30th the scene was staged in the Italian Parliament of shouted revendications against France. On January 2, 1939, Ciano informed Ribbentrop, both over the telephone and by a personal letter, that the Duce waived his previous reservations regarding the time for concluding the military alliance, and offered to have it signed towards the end of the month. In June Ribbentrop had affirmed that German preoccupations in Czechoslovakia did not enter into his proposal; now the Italians denied any connexion between their claims against France and their offer: they were prompted by "the proved existence of a Franco-British military pact," by "warlike tendencies in responsible French circles," and by "the military preparations of the United States." The treaty was "to be presented to the world as a peace pact." Thus within two months, and for no cogent reasons, everything was turned topsy-turvy. In 1917–1918 it used to be said in light-hearted Vienna that the situation in Austria was desperate but not serious. Hitler, too, and

Mussolini, Ribbentrop and Ciano were desperately dangerous, but not serious; as is seen in the negotiations which led up to the conclusion of the Pact of Steel.

Ribbentrop thought that by the end of January a tripartite treaty, including Japan, could be ready for signature; and he described it to Attolico as "one of the greatest events in history." Attolico put to him two *desiderata,* to be treated not as conditions but as "essential requests" (Ciano thought that he made too much of them): the one concerned "greater correctness in economic relations," and the other the Alto Adige (an announcement of population transfer was to put an end to all doubts). On January 6 Attolico was given a new draft of the pact, approved by the Führer. The overt treaty reproduced the Japanese draft of October 1938, with its reference in the preamble to "the strengthening of the defences against the Communist corrosion"; while the secret annexe set up an elaborate (and obscure) system of joint commissions. The only amendment to this draft suggested by Mussolini was to delete the phrase about "Communist corrosion."

Delays ensued; the Japanese Foreign Minister and the Admiralty were opposed to the alliance urged by the Army and its representatives in Berlin and Rome: Japan might have accepted the treaty if enabled to restrict its application to Russia, but would not engage simultaneously on a second front against the Anglo-Saxon Powers. Shiratori, Japanese Ambassador to Rome, explained to Attolico

that no Japanese Government could ever accept so vague a treaty of alliance. . . . A military strengthening of the Anti-Comintern Pact would be interpreted as referring foremost, if not exclusively, to war against the U.S.S.R. But this was naturally of limited interest to the European totalitarian Powers; hence a detailed definition was required of the cases covered by the treaty; what would Germany and Italy have to do in case of a conflict between Japan and Russia, or Japan of one between England and Germany or between Italy and France? What would Germany and Italy have to do in case of war between Japan and America? etc., etc. All this would have to be foreseen and exactly stated in the treaty. But for this — and he did not doubt the final result — time was required, and the European Powers, accustomed to correspond or negotiate over the telephone, should understand that the same methods could not be applied to Japan.

Ciano, after reading these remarks, noted in his *Diary*, on March 6, apparently oblivious of his own previous strictures on diplomacy by telephone:

. . . is it really possible to bring distant Japan so deeply into European life, which is becoming more and more convulsed and nervous and liable to be changed from hour to hour by a telephone call?

And two days later, with the same lack of self-critical humour:

The delays and procedure of the Japanese make me doubt the possibility of effective collaboration between Fascist and Nazi *dinamismo* and the phlegmatic slowness of Japan.

A few days later Hitler entered Prague, and started to redraw the map of Europe without any reference to his partner in "dynamics." What had become of Mussolini's presumed ascendancy at Munich? It was not the Czechoslovakia of the Paris Peace Treaties, but of the Munich settlement and of the Vienna Award of which Mussolini claimed paternity, that Hitler was destroying. Moreover, developments in Slovakia reacted on Croatia, and German activities were reported from Zagreb. Ciano made serious representations to the German Ambassador, and on March 18 Attolico wrote to Rome about the need of "a fundamental clarification": was there equality of rights and obligations between the Axis Powers, and what did the Germans make of the elementary duty of informing and consulting their partner? Was Italy to be excluded from the Balkans, with "only *the waters of the Mediterranean* reserved to

her"? Ciano deeply resented Hitler's action, and so at first did Mussolini; who next concluded that German hegemony was henceforth established in Europe, and, moreover, that Italy could not play "the prostitute" by changing her policy. On March 20 Ribbentrop, in a personal letter to Ciano, thanked Italy for her attitude, "full of understanding and friendship," and offered lame excuses for Germany's sudden "unpremeditated" decisions; he repeated the Führer's assurance that in all Mediterranean questions "the policy of the Axis shall be determined by Rome, and that Germany will therefore never pursue in Mediterranean countries a policy independent of Italy." Ciano replied by a short and dry letter — and this was all there was of Italian ill-humour. The mere fact that London reacted to Hitler's entry into Prague by attempts to build up a defensive front against aggression based on the "democratic Powers," drew Mussolini nearer to Hitler, while Ciano, who had long panted for his very own adventure in Albania, knew that he needed German support; *dinamismo* forced Italy into a position of dependency on Germany, and Ciano himself bears a heavy responsibility for Spain, Albania, and the attack on Greece. There was never to be "a true and proper clarification" of Axis relations, writes Professor Toscano.

No problem was thoroughly discussed. No precise obligations were formulated or assumed, and, barring Ribbentrop's letter, things were committed to uncertain memory, and not to paper. The ambiguity of Italo-German relations . . . was more than ever incurable. Hitler was not interested in clarifying them, while Mussolini feared the consequences of a thorough clarification.

On April 7 Italy invaded Albania. On the 13th the Western Powers announced their guarantees to Rumania and Greece; and they were negotiating with Russia and Turkey: these were developments that affected the sphere of interests claimed by Italy in the Balkans. On April 28 Hitler delivered a speech directed against Britain and Poland, but without a single hostile reference to Soviet Russia. Japan, however, insisted on giving the tripartite military alliance an exclusively anti-Russian character. This might have made Russia join the Western Powers, which would not have suited Germany's book. Hence, in spite of Ribbentrop's reluctance to shelve his *Weltpolitik*, by the end of April serious negotiations were confined to the two Axis Powers.

On April 14 Göring arrived in Rome. The upshot of several windy and verbose talks was to emphasize German-Italian solidarity; the inevitability of a conflict with the Western Powers; the need of both Axis Powers for an interval in which to complete their armaments; and Germany's determination to solve the Polish problem. There was an obvious and disquieting contradiction between the last two propositions; this made the Italians urgently seek direct contact with Ribbentrop, who in reply suggested a meeting with Ciano at Como between May 6 and 8; he would bring with him a draft of the German-Italian pact. Attolico telegraphed on May 2 a warning against negotiating such a pact "in a hurry and, as it were, *stante pede*."

A pact limited to Italy and Germany could not be a vague document, such as that prepared by Japan. It needs to be more precise, take account of certain indispensable premises (the Brenner frontier: solution of the German problem in the Alto Adige), acknowledge the right of either side to its own *Lebensraum*, and define the limits and modes of interpretation of interests in mixed zones, confirming our right to an equal share in trade and expansion in the Balkans and the Danube Basin, etc., etc.

Further, in view of past experience, a treaty of alliance with Germany would have to fix clearly the extent of obligatory mutual consultation in all matters of common interest....

Similarly, an Italo-German pact would have to enter much more thoroughly into military details than a vague tripartite pact reinforcing the anti-Comintern agreement. But all this cannot be improvised and would have to be quietly prepared. . . .

Attolico knew only too well the two men to whom he was preaching, and preaching in vain.

On May 4 Attolico reported that the Legal Department of the German Foreign Office had been instructed to prepare the draft of a dual alliance; and the same day Mussolini gave Ciano instructions for his talks with Ribbentrop. "It is my firm conviction," he wrote, "that the two European Powers of the Axis require a period of peace of at least three years. It is only after 1943 that a war effort will have the best prospects of victory." Italy had to organize Libya and Albania for war, and pacify Abyssinia which would be able to raise an army of half a million men; reconstruct her navy and re-equip her artillery; develop economic autarchy, cash in the foreign money which the Exhibition of 1942 was expected to attract, repatriate the Italians from France, and transfer many of her war industries from the Po Valley to the south; lastly, strengthen the ties between the two Axis nations, which would be greatly helped by a *détente* between the Church and Nazism, "much desired by the Vatican." "For all these reasons Fascist Italy does not desire to hasten a European war, though convinced of its being unavoidable." In a further *tour d'horizon*, Mussolini spoke of his agreement with Britain as formal rather than substantial, and as "of negative rather than of positive application." "In case of a war limited to Italy and France, the Italian Government does not ask for German help in men but merely in *matériel*." He admitted an understanding with Russia to the extent of keeping her out of a hostile *bloc*, but beyond that it would be misunderstood within the Axis countries and would weaken their connexion. What Mussolini really apprehended was that an understanding between Germany and Russia would reduce still farther Italy's rôle in the alliance.

On May 5 the French Press published reports of bloody anti-German demonstrations in Milan: whereupon Mussolini had the Ciano-Ribbentrop meeting transferred from Como to Milan. When the two met the next day Ribbentrop's talk was obliging and inconclusive (and even what he said was never fixed in an agreed minute): in Poland, time is working for Germany; the Poles are megalomaniacs, with no sense of reality; France and England are getting tired of them, and soon no one will be prepared to go to war over Poland; Germany does not mean "to take the first step," but of course if provoked "will react in the sharpest manner"; Germany, too, is convinced of the need for peace for a period of "not less than four or five years," but if war is forced on her, etc. He promised to send the draft for a treaty of alliance to be signed with great solemnity in Berlin.

At night Mussolini had the truly original idea of having the pact announced before its terms were settled, and telephoned accordingly to Ciano. Ribbentrop, who still hankered after the inclusion of Japan, demurred, but telephoned to Hitler who agreed; whereupon an official announcement was prepared and published: the relations of the two Axis States were to be fixed definitely and formally by means of a political and military pact. That announcement, writes Professor Toscano, "could serve as an excellent means of diplomatic pressure on France. They were playing with fire, but this had become a habit. . . ."

On May 12, the draft treaty was given to Attolico with the suggestion of signing some time between May 21 and 24.

The German and the Italian peoples, closely bound to each other by the deep affinity of their ways of life and the complete solidarity of their interests, have determined in future to stand guard side by side and with united forces over their eternal rights to life and over the maintenance of peace.

. . . .

Should it happen that, contrary to the wishes and hopes of the Contracting Parties, one of them was involved in war . . . the other will place itself immediately as ally at its side, and support it with all its forces by land, on sea, and in the air.

No time-limit was set to the duration of that treaty, between "National-Socialist Germany and Fascist Italy," although revisions were foreseen without indication of date. In a secret annexe special provisions were made for cooperation in matters of Press and propaganda.

Attolico pointed out in his comments that the Brenner frontier was nowhere mentioned; that the customary formula about "unprovoked aggression" was dropped, enjoining the completest solidarity, offensive no less than defensive; and that the expression "eternal rights to life" lent itself "to the most varied alarmist interpretations." He suggested that at least in the title a defensive character should be ascribed to the treaty; and that quinquennial periods of revision should be fixed. (As Professor Toscano points out, the automatism of support to a high degree stultified the consultation clause, and, given Germany's superiority, was bound "in its improvident latitude" to work against Italy.)

"I have never read such a pact," Ciano wrote in his Diary. "It is real and proper dynamite." Attolico was authorized to put forward amendments concerning the Alto Adige and periods of revision — otherwise that extraordinary draft was accepted without demur: after having talked of the need of peace for at least three years, Mussolini left it to Hitler to start war whenever he chose, with Italy bound to range herself immediately by his side, no matter how or why the war had been started. And only after the "Pact of Steel" had been signed in Berlin with much flourish on May 22 did he bethink himself of establishing its exact bearing.

On May 21 Mussolini sent General Cavallero to Hitler with a memorandum putting his own interpretation on the pact. The document reproduces in full Ciano's instructions shown to Ribbentrop at Milan, which gave at great length Mussolini's reasons for wishing to see peace preserved for at least three years. The rest (including a paragraph about weakening the internal unity of enemy States by means of anti-Semitic, pacifist, or regionalist movements, or by revolts in their colonies) was window-dressing: what Mussolini sought was the Führer's official approval for his time-table, which would have made it the basis for directives to be prepared by the two General Staffs. But Hitler merely thanked him in a verbal message for his note, declared "in principle" his agreement with its argument, and expressed the wish to talk over matters personally with Mussolini. On May 23, the day after the Pact of Steel had been signed, Hitler had decided "at the first suitable opportunity to attack Poland"; and on August 11 Ciano was informed by Ribbentrop at Salzburg that war was imminent. The Italians now wanted to protest (some even to cancel the pact); but when Ciano, on August 21, tried to arrange a further meeting with Ribbentrop, in order to clarify matters that should have been clarified before the pact was signed, he learnt that Ribbentrop was going to Moscow "to sign a political pact with the Soviet Government." "There is no doubt," wrote Ciano in his *Diary,* "the Germans have struck a master blow. The European situation is upset."

HISTORY'S CASE AGAINST HITLER:
AN AMERICAN VIEW

RAYMOND J. SONTAG

Professor of history at the University of California (Berkeley), Raymond J. Sontag won justified acclaim in the 1930's for a balanced account of the coming of World War I. It was especially fitting that a man of his competence in German diplomatic history was selected in 1946 to serve as United States representative on an American-British-French board of editors that was to select and publish captured documents of the German Foreign Office. Professor Sontag served as chief American editor from 1946 to 1949. With James A. Beddie, Sontag edited the documents the Department of State published in 1948 on *Nazi-Soviet Relations, 1939–1941.* Under able successors the documents on Germany's 1939 diplomacy were completely published in 1956. They provided a basis for an article by Sontag in *Foreign Affairs*, from which this reading is taken. Clearly and without resort to emotionalism, Sontag shows how Hitler pressed his Polish demands until he pushed himself and Europe into war.

HITLER freely admitted [before September, 1939] that his successes in the foreign field had been won by bluff. The conviction was general in Europe that the First World War had dangerously undermined European society and that another war would bring the structure to ruin, with Communism as the only gainer. The Soviet Union, sharing this conviction, was eager to stand clear so that it would not be involved in the general ruin. By exploiting fear of war Hitler had won much. He was confident that still more must be won by diplomacy before he could safely embark on war with the West.

Some day, Hitler recognized, Britain and France would be tempted to set limits to German power, even by war. In preparation for that day, he argued, Germany must not only strain her resources in military preparations; she must also win territory sufficient to feed her people during a long war — for war with the Western democracies would be both long and hard. Colonies would be of no value; their resources would be lost by blockade just when they were needed. The territory must be won in Eastern Europe. There, German skill could increase agricultural production, and the non-German population would provide a labor pool for farm and factory. The moment was, he believed, auspicious. Russia could not interfere: the purges had shaken the country and deprived the Red Army of its leaders; Stalin must fear a victorious army no less than military defeat. Fear of Russia would hold Poland on the side of Germany so long as exactions from Poland were counterbalanced by concessions to Polish territorial greed. Italy and Japan were so completely estranged from the Western democracies that they must follow the German lead. British and especially French rearmament was only beginning,

From Raymond J. Sontag, "The Last Months of Peace, 1939," *Foreign Affairs*, XXXV (April, 1957), pp. 508–515, 519–524. Reprinted by permission of *Foreign Affairs*. Copyrighted by the Council on Foreign Relations, Inc., New York.

and was encountering opposition unavoidable where the press was unmuzzled. Above all, Britain and France were ruled by men who had already retreated before the threat of war. Hitler was convinced that they lacked the resolution to precipitate a war or conduct it to the death.

The moves of March 1939 were, like the annexation of Austria and the Sudeten districts of Czechoslovakia, merely preliminary to the task of winning "living space." They would provide better frontiers and advanced military bases in the east, jumping-off places for future action. They would not bring the enlarged agricultural base needed for the future long war of annihilation with the Western democracies. Hitler made no diplomatic or military preparations which would suggest that even local opposition of any importance was anticipated. In one sense he envisioned the moves of March 1939 as the logical completion of the campaign against Czechoslovakia; in another sense, they were moves preparatory to the winning of the desired agricultural base.

In the early morning hours of March 15, 1939, after a stormy interview with Hitler, President Hácha wearily signed away the independence of what was left of Czechoslovakia. German troops had already crossed the frontier, and by afternoon Hitler was in Prague. The following Monday, March 20, the Lithuanian Foreign Minister was received by Ribbentrop and told that Memel must be surrendered to Germany. Even before this demand was accepted on Thursday, the next move was made.

On Tuesday, March 21, Ribbentrop asked the Polish Ambassador, Lipski, to call on him. The Ambassador said that the German protectorate over Slovakia had hit Poland hard. Ribbentrop hinted that the status of Slovakia was not necessarily final and might be subject to discussion if German-Polish relations developed satisfactorily. It was Hitler's hope, Ribbentrop continued, that such would be the case; but the Führer was troubled by anti-German

feeling in Poland. The Poles must surely recognize that unless they cooperated with Germany they would be absorbed by Communist Russia. It was necessary to put German-Polish relations on a sound and lasting basis. To this end, Danzig must return to Germany, and Germany must be granted extra-territorial rail and road connections between the Reich and East Prussia. Then Hitler would be prepared to guarantee the Polish Corridor, and then it would be possible to deal with the Slovak question to the satisfaction of all. Ribbentrop suggested that Lipski take these proposals to Warsaw. Possibly the Polish Foreign Minister, Beck, would come to Berlin to discuss them; Hitler would warmly welcome such a discussion.

Lipski did go to Warsaw, and while he was away Hitler informed his army commander that a military solution of the problem of Danzig was not desired, because this would drive Poland into the arms of Britain; the use of Slovakia as a bargaining counter to win Polish agreement was contemplated. While he did not wish to solve the Polish question militarily unless especially favorable political conditions arose, Hitler continued, plans should be made, with the objective of beating the Poles so thoroughly that they would not be a political factor for some decades. He would absent himself from Berlin, leaving the conduct of negotiations with Lipski to Ribbentrop.

The Polish reply was presented by Lipski on Sunday, March 26. In form it was most conciliatory, but it did not meet the German demands. Ribbentrop, from his discussion with Lipski, drew the conclusion that this was not the Polish Government's last word and that Poland merely wished to escape as cheaply as possible. The next day, he applied pressure. The Polish reply, he said, could not be regarded as a basis for a settlement; German-Polish relations were, therefore, deteriorating rapidly. Lipski promised to do what he could to overcome the difficulties. Two days later, the German representative in Danzig was told that

Poland was not to be provoked. Polish reluctance would be worn down by attrition tactics, and Danzig should adopt a sphinx-like attitude. Ribbentrop was of the opinion that the climax of the crisis had been reached.

Already signs were multiplying that the crisis was not, in fact, at its climax, and that Prague, Memel and Danzig had violently shaken world diplomatic alignments. In Britain and France the annihilation of Czechoslovakia produced a strong popular reaction against the policy of appeasement. Chamberlain and Daladier had wavered and then fallen in with the popular mood. Recognition of the German action in Czechoslovakia was refused, and the British and French Ambassadors in Berlin were ordered home for consultation. When there were rumors of new German moves in Central Europe, there was a flurry of diplomatic activity from which emerged, on March 31, a declaration by Chamberlain in the House of Commons that Britain and France would aid Poland in resisting any action clearly threatening Polish independence. Hard on this declaration, the Polish Foreign Minister arrived in London, and at the conclusion of his visit Chamberlain stated on April 6 that a permanent alliance would be negotiated between Britain and Poland. Moreover, Chamberlain offered similar guarantees to states of southeastern Europe, and these offers met with a sympathetic reception despite German reminders that "the shelter of the umbrella" had been no protection for Abyssinia, Austria, Czechoslovakia or the Spanish Republicans. More ominous, negotiations began in mid-April for drawing the Soviet Union into what the Germans called the British encirclement program; someone kept the German Embassy in London fully and promptly informed of these negotiations. Finally, even the United States Government assumed a more active rôle. At the onset of the March crisis, the German chargé in Washington warned that the Roosevelt Administration was determined to support Britain and France in any war with Germany and that, while American opinion was opposed to war, this opposition would collapse on the first news of air attacks on British or French cities. On April 15, President Roosevelt appealed directly to Hitler and Mussolini, asking for assurance against armed attack on a long list of states.

Even within the Axis, the occupation of Prague produced a violent reaction. As usual, the Italian Government had received no advance notice of the German action, and repetition intensified Italian resentment against such cavalier treatment. Now, however, the Italians were not only humiliated; they were frightened. Austria and Czechoslovakia were completely under German control, and Hungary was a dependent of the Reich. As a reliable informant told the Germans, "people are saying that in the end the old Hapsburg Empire, this time under the swastika flag, will reappear on the Adriatic." German assurances that the Mediterranean, including the Adriatic, was an Italian sphere of influence, did not disarm Italian fears. On Good Friday, Mussolini moved to solidify the Italian position by seizing Albania, and he did not forewarn Germany. Meanwhile, more and more clearly the Italian suggestion that Germans in the South Tyrol be resettled in Germany was changing to a firm demand. Italian policy was assuming an unaccustomed and potentially dangerous independence of German leadership.

There is no evidence that all this activity caused Hitler any alarm, and much evidence that he continued confident of success. As the weeks passed, German policy towards Poland changed, and by May 23 Hitler was resolved to attack her at the first suitable opportunity; but this was to be an isolated operation, from which other Powers would remain aloof.

By April 3, when Beck arrived in London, it was already obvious that the German plan to hold Poland away from Britain had failed. On the same day, the high command of the Wehrmacht was instructed to prepare plans for an attack on Poland in such a way that the operation could begin at any time from September 1. In the amplification of these instructions issued on April 11, the war with Poland was still described as a possibility to be avoided if possible; in any case, every precaution must be taken to limit the war to Poland only. The proposal made by Ribbentrop to Lipski was withdrawn on April 6; German missions abroad were instructed not to discuss the proposal or the Polish counteroffer.

The war of nerves was begun, with full confidence of victory. Ribbentrop was convinced that "not one British soldier would be mobilized in the event of a German-Polish conflict." Göring and Hitler expressed the same conviction. Public excitement, the Nazis argued, had pushed Beck, Chamberlain and Daladier into foolish threats and promises, but, as Hitler said, "one could only yell for a certain time." When passions cooled, and reason reasserted itself, it would become obvious that the German position was overwhelmingly strong. In the German view, British and French rearmament had only begun, and the German West Wall was impregnable; therefore no effective help could come to Poland from the west. Russia would not fight, and in any case the Poles knew that the Russians, if they ever entered their country, would never leave. There were even signs that reason, as the Nazis understood reason, was returning. The French and British Ambassadors returned to their posts in Berlin; and the latter, Nevile Henderson, promised that he would not cease to work for a favorable solution. The German chargé in Warsaw reported that responsible Poles wished to keep the way open for a rapprochement, although they could do nothing because of the excited state of public opinion. The German chargé in Moscow stressed Soviet "mistrust and reserve" in relations with the West, and on April 17 the Soviet Ambassador in Berlin suggested that so far as the

U.S.S.R. was concerned, Nazi-Soviet relations could easily be improved. And so Hitler was probably quite honest when he said that he "had a great deal of time for theatres and concerts" and that he "regarded the whole course of events calmly."

Through four weeks after Chamberlain's promise of assistance to the Poles, the Germans kept their own counsel. Then, on Friday, April 28, Hitler spoke. The British encirclement policy and the Polish military agreement had, he said, destroyed the Anglo-German naval agreement of 1935 and the German-Polish political understanding of 1934. With irony verging on ridicule, he dismissed Roosevelt's peace appeal as meaningless. About Russia he said nothing. The reaction abroad to the speech, as reported by German representatives, was heartening. The comment of the chargé in Paris (the German Ambassadors to Britain and France had not yet returned to their posts) was typical: "It is fairly generally recognized that the tone of the speech was moderate, serious and dignified, and that the German demands are by no means incapable of being met."

A week after Hitler's speech the strength of the German position was dramatized by a meeting in Milan between Ribbentrop and the Italian Foreign Minister, Ciano. In the communiqué issued at the conclusion of the meeting, on May 7, emphasis was placed on the "perfect identity of views" between Germany and Italy, and on the intention of the two Governments to conclude a political and military pact — the pact which was grandiloquently to be called "The Pact of Steel."

Actually, the pact which was announced on May 7 and concluded on May 22 was thought a poor and temporary substitute for the alliance of Germany, Italy and Japan for which the Germans had been pressing. The Japanese were willing to conclude an alliance against Russia; they were as yet unwilling to promise military assistance against Britain and the United States. Since the alliance was wanted by

Hitler as a means of bringing the British to a more "reasonable" attitude, the proposal of an alliance against Russia was rejected. As an alternative, Ribbentrop touched lightly in his discussion with Ciano on the possibility of improving relations with the Soviet Union. Ciano thought such a move desirable; but felt that for domestic political reasons Mussolini would not wish too great an improvement.

At this stage in the developing crisis, the Germans also showed no great eagerness to strengthen their position by bidding for the support of the Soviet Union, despite clear indications of the importance which the British and French attached to a political agreement with the U.S.S.R. When Dirksen returned to his post in London he reported that failure to achieve agreement with Russia would shake the position of the British. Similarly, on his return to Paris, Welczeck reported that "even right-wing circles are convinced that without Russia there would be no possibility of effectively stemming the German advance in the East."

The Russians did their best to elicit a German offer. On May 3 Molotov replaced Litvinov as Foreign Secretary and the Soviet chargé in Berlin intimated that the change could facilitate improvement in Nazi-Soviet relations. Two weeks later he again suggested that an improvement in relations would not be difficult to achieve. The German Government did bring Schulenburg, the Ambassador in Moscow, home for consultation; but he returned to Russia with instructions only to suggest the reopening of economic negotiations which had been interrupted earlier in the year. Schulenburg talked with Molotov for over an hour on May 20, but found him unwilling to reopen the economic discussions until a "political basis" had been found. After some wavering, the German Government decided to make no definite political proposals.

On May 23, Hitler reviewed the international situation with his military advisers. Now, two months after his first demands on Poland, he had enlarged his objective.

Poland was to be attacked at the first suitable opportunity, and destroyed. "It is not Danzig that is at stake. For us it is a matter of expanding our living space in the East and making food supplies secure and also solving the problem of the Baltic States." The campaign against Poland could be a success only if Britain and France stood aside. There were indications that "Russia might disinterest herself in the destruction of Poland," but to restrain Russia it might be necessary to have closer ties with Japan. In any case, the task was to isolate Poland, and there must not be a simultaneous showdown with France and Britain. That showdown would come, but later. It would be a hard, and probably a long fight, involving the very existence of Germany; it was time to begin preparations for that fight. He was, therefore, setting up a small planning staff, which would work in complete secrecy, and which would study all aspects of the problem of preparing for the life and death battle with Britain. He gave no date for the war with the West, but in response to a question from Göring he stated that the armaments program would be completed by 1943 or 1944. (pp. 515-519)

One cannot say with certainty that Hitler was forced to revise his policy towards Russia by recognition that time was running out. What is certain is that while Hitler had ordered efforts to secure even a trade agreement stopped on June 29, and while opinion within the German Government was still fluctuating two weeks later, the pace was rapidly accelerated in the days following the uproar in Britain over the supposed offer of a huge loan to Germany by the Chamberlain government. The official in charge of the economic negotiations, Schnurre, wrote privately on August 2 that, from about July 23, he had at least one conversation daily about Russia with Ribbentrop who was also constantly exchanging views with Hitler. "The Foreign Minister is concerned to obtain some result in the Russian question as soon as possible, not only on the negative side (disturbing the British negotiations) but also on the

cf. Taylor

positive side (an understanding with us).

During the weeks which followed, the Nazis were driven, step by step, to meet every Soviet demand. The first step, on July 26, was a long dinner conversation, extending past midnight, between Schnurre, the Soviet chargé and the Soviet trade representative. Emphasizing that he was speaking on Ribbentrop's instructions, Schnurre declared that there was no real conflict of interest between Germany and the U.S.S.R. at any point from the Baltic to the Black Sea and on to the Far East, and said he "could imagine a far-reaching arrangement of mutual interests" in all these areas. However, he warned, the opportunity to effect such an arrangement would be lost if the U.S.S.R. allied itself with Britain. The Russians expressed surprise and pleasure at these remarks; they reciprocated Schnurre's desire for improved relations, but emphasized that improvement could come only slowly.

A week later, on August 2, Ribbentrop intervened directly. In conversation with the Soviet chargé, he reiterated the German conviction that a far-reaching political agreement was possible and "dropped a gentle hint at our coming to an understanding with Russia on the fate of Poland." The chargé tried to elicit information on the concrete terms Ribbentrop had in mind; the latter said he was quite ready to be explicit when the Soviet Government stated that it also wished to put relations on a new basis.

During the days which followed, the German representatives repeatedly sought to draw from the Russians a definite statement of willingness to enter negotiations on political problems, but without success. At last, on August 10, Schnurre came to the point. He stressed the impossibility of any agreement if the U.S.S.R. concluded a military pact with Britain. Beyond that, however, he made it plain that war against Poland impended, and that a demarcation of spheres of interest in Poland was desirable before war came. This produced results. Two days later, the chargé reported that his government was interested in a discussion of political problems, including Poland, and wished the negotiations to take place in Moscow.

To Hitler it seemed that the road ahead was now clear. In a conference at Obersalzberg on August 14 he stated categorically that Russia would keep out of the war. Britain would, in the end, draw back: "the men I got to know in Munich are not the kind that start a new World War." Without Britain, France would not move.

That evening, Ribbentrop telegraphed new proposals to Schulenburg, proposals which he wished Stalin to receive in as exact a form as was possible without putting an incriminating document into Soviet hands. He proposed a linking of the Soviet and German economies, "which are complementary in every sphere." He proposed political cooperation. He affirmed "that there is no question between the Baltic Sea and the Black Sea which cannot be settled to the complete satisfaction of both countries." To secure speedy agreement, he was prepared to come to Moscow himself "to lay the foundations for a final settlement of German-Russian relations."

By then, the September 1 deadline was less than three weeks away and the propaganda campaign preparatory to war with Poland was already approaching its strident climax. Foreign observers in Berlin were freely predicting that the question of Danzig if not the fate of Poland would be settled before the month was over. Hitler encouraged these prophets. In the past he had carefully concealed his plan of action from the indiscreet Italians. This time, he was very explicit. War against Poland might come any day, he told Ciano, and would come by the end of August unless Poland not only surrendered Danzig but altered "her general attitude."

German need was Russian opportunity. Even while they had suggested ever more plainly their desire for a political agreement with Germany, the Russians had continued their negotiations with the British and French. At the time that he had announced the opening of trade negotiations with Germany, Molotov had also suggested the sending of an Anglo-French military mission to Moscow as a means of speeding agreement with the Western democracies. The discussions of this mission with the Soviet military leaders were begun on the very day, August 12, that the Germans were told of Soviet willingness to begin political discussions. Now, on August 15, when Schulenburg presented Ribbentrop's proposal that he come to Moscow, Molotov stressed the need for "adequate preparation" before the arrival of so distinguished a visitor and asked whether Germany was prepared to conclude a nonaggression pact and to influence Japanese policy in the direction of better relations with the Soviet Union.

Two days later — and even this short interval seemed long to Ribbentrop — Schulenburg was back with fresh instructions. Germany would conclude a nonaggression pact. Germany was willing to influence Japanese policy in the desired direction. But speed was essential because "of the possibility of the occurrence, any day, of serious events." Ribbentrop was prepared to come to Moscow by airplane at any time after August 18. Molotov refused to be hurried, and laid out a timetable: first the economic agreement must be concluded; then "after a short interval" a political agreement could be made; however, there might now be an exchange of drafts of the proposed political agreement, and the Soviet Government would await with interest the German draft.

Promptly, Schulenburg received new instructions, which he executed in two interviews with Molotov on August 19. With only the thinnest covering of diplomatic verbiage, the Russians were told that war was imminent and that a delineation of spheres of influence was essential before the fighting started. In the first interview Molotov refused to set a date for Ribbentrop's visit. In the second, Molotov (apparently on new instructions from Stalin)

agreed that Ribbentrop might come on August 26 or 27. Meanwhile, in Berlin, the trade agreement was finally signed.

Hitler now intervened with a letter to Stalin. Polish presumption, said Hitler, had produced intolerable tension which might lead to war any day. There was no time to lose. He asked that Ribbentrop be received on August 22, or at the latest on August 23; Ribbentrop would have full powers to draw up and sign the nonaggression pact and the political agreement. The letter was delivered on August 21. On the same day Stalin replied, agreeing to the arrival of Ribbentrop on August 23. That night, the German Government issued a communiqué telling of the impending conference for the purpose of concluding a nonaggression pact.

The final card had been played. It was a costly move. At the end of May, consideration for Soviet interests in Poland had been the highest price mentioned for a pact with the U.S.S.R. As late as August 16 Ribbentrop offered, so far as the Baltic States were concerned, only a joint guarantee of their independence. Now, in the pact of August 23, Finland, Estonia and Latvia were to be an exclusively Soviet sphere of influence. Russia was also to receive a large share of Poland. As for southeastern Europe, the Soviet claim to Bessarabia was acknowledged, while "the German side declares complete political *désintéressement* in these territories." In the search for "living space," a search which had seemed so easy in the spring, Hitler had been forced to surrender his claim to hegemony in the Baltic and in southeastern Europe.

The cost was high, but again Hitler was confident that he could now crush Poland without provoking general war. On August 22, before Ribbentrop reached Moscow, Hitler called his military leaders together once more. Most of what he said was an elaborate demonstration of the necessity for war with Poland, together with instructions for the ruthless conduct of the war. So far as Britain and France were concerned, his arguments were those he had used so often before: neither had really rearmed, both were obsessed by the frightful risks entailed by war, neither had strong leaders. He said the German attack would probably be launched on Saturday, August 26.

Momentarily, Hitler's optimism seemed justified by reports of the confusion caused in Britain and France by the Nazi-Soviet pact. On Wednesday, August 23, the attack on Poland was definitely set for Saturday, and on August 24 the first of the moves by which war was to be provoked was made by the Germans in Danzig. On August 25, however, there came two heavy blows: the Anglo-Polish Mutual Assistance Agreement was signed, and Mussolini made it plain that he would not intervene if Germany became involved in war with France and Britain. In the evening, the order to attack was cancelled.

There followed a week of desperate manoeuvring. Much has been written of the "offers" made by Hitler in those last days of peace, but it is now clear that the offers were intended only to shake the determination of the British Government. Hitler had gone too far to retreat, and time had run out. On September 1, the German invasion began, with Hitler still vainly hoping that the political leaders of Britain and France would, at the last moment, lose their nerve.

Over and over, through the spring and summer of 1939 the British and French Governments had said they would fight if Germany attacked Poland. These warnings went unheeded. In justification for his refusal to heed the warnings from London and Paris, Hitler invariably came back to the same arguments: Britain and France were militarily unprepared for war, and certainly for a war to protect Poland; they had threatened before, and had drawn back at the end; the men in power in 1939 were the same men whose will had collapsed in face of firm resistance. As he repeatedly boasted, he had bluffed and won before; what he had done when Germany was weak, he could do again with confidence now that Germany was strong.

These boasts had an increasingly hollow sound from the last week of July. But by then the whole world had come to regard the question of Danzig as a decisive test of strength. Through the years since 1933 he had advanced from one victory to another by convincing his opponents that if they did not surrender he would annihilate them and, if necessary, bring what Bonnet called the house of Europe crashing in ruins. Now Hitler was confronted by the despised Poles; they not only remained steady through the war of nerves, but, despite all provocation, they avoided rash action which would place the onus of aggression on them. If they were able to defy him with impunity, the tide which had carried him from success to success would turn. In a last desperate effort to break the will of his opponents, he promised the hated Communists more for neutrality than he could win from war against Poland. Even under this pressure the courage of the Poles did not collapse. Retreat was now more impossible than ever. And so the diplomatic moves of March, intended at the outset only to advance Germany another stage along the road to supremacy in Europe, led inexorably, step by step, to war against the West in which the very existence of Germany was at stake.

HISTORY'S CASE AGAINST HITLER: A GERMAN VIEW

HERMANN MAU AND HELMUT KRAUSNICK

The case against Hitler for causing the Second World War has been made by distinguished historians of Germany as well as by Western historians. In 1953 Hermann Mau and Helmut Krausnick of the Institut für Zeitgeschichte (Institute for Contemporary History) originally published the account of the Third Reich from which this reading was taken. In 1961, when many questions were being raised in England and the United States about how Germans viewed their own recent history, an English translation of the Mau-Krausnick volume was published. By then Dr. Mau had died prematurely as a result of an automobile accident, but Professor Krausnick and many other West German historians—young and old—have continued to strive for objective interpretations of Germany's recent history. Governmental offices of the Bonn Republic have seen to it that their appraisals are circulated in the public schools of West Germany. A survey in 1960–1961 of history textbooks used in West German elementary and high schools showed that most of them presented interpretations akin to those Mau and Krausnick offered in 1953. (Karl Mielcke, *1917–1945 in den Geschichtsbüchern der Bundesrepublik* [Hannover, 1961], 73–76, 114–115, 148–150.) In East Germany (the "German Democratic Republic") historians have slavishly followed the interpretations offered by the U.S.S.R.

THE snatch at Prague was a fateful event. It proved the decisive turning-point in Hitler's career and unleashed developments leading directly to the war and eventually to the abyss. The agreement at Munich, to which the Western Powers had given their consent only on the tacit assumption that this was Hitler's last territorial demand and that he would keep the peace in future, was cynically torn up. The world at last realised that the revision of the Treaty of Versailles and Hitler's evocation of the right of self-determination were only pretexts for an imperialist policy of conquest. In Austria and the Sudetenland the Reich had acquired territories which were linguistically and ethnically German.

In the "Protectorate of Bohemia and Moravia" it had for the first time, and contrary to all Nazi theories, annexed foreign nationalities.

The end of Czechoslovakia brought the danger zone of Nazi aggression closer towards Poland. Between Germany and Poland stood a problem dating from long before 1933: Danzig and the question of the Polish Corridor. A sensible revision of this unsatisfactory arrangement, with which the Polish need for free access to the sea had been satisfied at Versailles, was a German concern for which the Treaty Powers entertained a certain sympathy. But after Prague nobody could keep up the belief that Hitler was merely interested in sensi-

From Hermann Mau and Helmut Krausnick, *German History, 1933–45: An Assessment by German Historians,* transl. by Andrew and Eva Wilson (London, 1961). Reprinted by permission of Oswald Wolff (Publishers) Ltd.

ble revisions. The reaction of the European Powers to the aggressive attitude which Hitler began to adopt towards Poland was marked by the conviction that Hitler's aim was not the revisions he demanded but the conquest of "living space" in the East.

Covered by the German-Polish Treaty of 1934, Hitler had left the Polish question undisturbed as long as he needed Poland's neutrality. After the annexation of Austria and Czechoslovakia he saw no further reason for consideration. Within a few weeks of Munich he informed Poland that the time had come to settle old issues. On October 24th 1938 Ribbentrop told Lipski, the Polish Ambassador in Berlin, that Germany wished to discuss a "general settlement" of all problems between the two countries. Germany demanded the return of Danzig and the construction of an extra-territorial traffic route through the Corridor. Warsaw rejected this first German advance out of hand. After the German occupation of Prague the German Foreign Minister renewed his Government's demands with greater urgency, and diplomatic discussions between Germany and Poland now turned upon these questions with increasing acrimony, with Poland clinging tenaciously to her original attitude.

The tension caused by Germany's demands and their consistent rejection by the Polish Government ceased to be a purely German-Polish problem. It resulted in the formation of broad political fronts which were to become, within a few months, war fronts.

On the opposing side Great Britain assumed political leadership. Prague had led to a radical renunciation of the policy of appeasement of which Munich had become the symbol. It was Chamberlain himself, the most ardent champion of appeasement, who made this change in British foreign policy. Ever since Prague, Britain had become convinced that Hitler was trying to eliminate her influence on the Continent in order to have a free hand in the East, and that he was seeking European hegemony. In March 1939 Britain tried to obtain a joint Anglo-French-Polish-Soviet guarantee for all European states whose independence might be threatened in the future. The attempt failed through Poland's eternal reluctance to collaborate with the Soviet Union. As a result, Britain gave Poland a unilateral guarantee at the end of March, to which Poland responded a few days later with a similar guarantee to Britain. By declaring her solidarity, France reactivated her old treaty of 1921 with Poland, which in the shadow of the German-Polish Treaty of 1934 had become politically ineffective. The British guarantee to Poland was followed in April by similar declarations to Rumania and Greece.

On April 28th Hitler countered the British initiative by abrogating the Anglo-German Naval Agreement of 1935 and the German-Polish Treaty of 1934, regardless of the fact that neither agreement permitted abrogation without notice. From now on, German propaganda accused Great Britain of pursuing a policy of encirclement, thereby awakening, in Germany, disquieting memories. At the same time, adopting the formulae used in the preparation of the Sudeten crisis the year before, it accused the Polish Government of terrorising its German minorities. In May Hitler managed to confirm the collaboration of the Berlin-Rome "axis" in a formal military alliance, which later, however, was to disappoint the expectations expressed by its official name, the "Pact of Steel." During these same weeks Denmark, Latvia and Estonia accepted German offers of non-aggression pacts. On the other side, England extended her promises of assistance to include Turkey.

Since the beginning of April the Wehrmacht had been in possession of directives for the event of a war with Poland. Preparations were to be accelerated so that it would be possible to commence operations "at any time from September 1st 1939 onwards." This did not mean that Hitler had decided to act, although he was to begin the war on exactly that date. Hitler realised that the Polish problem could no longer be treated in isolation — that upon it hung the whole peace of Europe. As in the case of Czechoslovakia, he was only going to march if he was certain of avoiding involvement in a war on two fronts. After the spring of 1939 his political efforts were therefore directed towards Poland's isolation. The Western Powers, on their side, were trying to weave Germany's eastern neighbours, particularly Poland and Rumania, into a comprehensive system of security pacts. As both sides pursued their diplomatic activities, the summer saw a dramatic race for the favour of the Soviet Union, on which each pinned its hopes of tipping the balance.

In March 1939 Britain and France had entered into *pourparlers* with Russia, since effective help to the smaller states of Eastern Europe seemed impossible without Russian participation. The Russians showed willingness. But there were difficulties in the way of formulating a joint plan. Britain wanted the Soviet Union merely to associate itself with the guarantees which she herself had given. Russia, on the other hand, suggested a Soviet-Anglo-French pact with much farther-reaching commitments. France was prepared to accept the Russian proposal. But Britain was against committing herself that far. For months proposals and counter-proposals passed to and fro. At last, on July 24th, a political pact was agreed upon which stipulated mutual assistance in the event of any of the three Powers being attacked, and which promised assistance to a number of smaller European states, including Poland and Rumania. England had gone thus far to meet Russian wishes at the anxious insistence of France. But the pact was a fiction, for it was only to come into force when agreement had been reached on a supplementary military convention. During the subsequent discussions, the military experts came up against the same difficulties which had beset the diplomats. The obstacle was the attitude of the smaller states. The Soviet Union demanded the right to march through Poland and Rumania, without which her military cooperation in defence against Nazi aggression was difficult to visualise. But both states refused to grant this right, fearing to compromise themselves irrevocably with Germany and at the same time to deliver themselves into the equally feared hands of the Soviet Union. Poland, in particular, considered her independence of the two (as she thought) irreconcilable Powers to be a positive political asset. Only under steady French pressure did she begin to show signs of cautious agreement. Just as the discussions seemed to be showing renewed promise, they were brought to a lamentable end by the sensational news of the German-Soviet non-aggression pact. Hitler had outstripped the Western Powers in equally long, but secret, discussions in Moscow.

The documents so far made public give no clear answer as to which side initiated the German-Soviet talks. After the spring of 1939 each seems to have had an inclination to put out feelers about the possibility of a German-Soviet understanding. The *rapprochement* proceeded slowly, in careful and suspicious diplomatic talks, which at first were concerned with economic relations, but were later extended by the Russians to include political questions. It was a sign of Russian seriousness that on May 5th, 1939 the representative of Soviet collaboration with the West, Litvinov, was replaced as Foreign Minister by Molotov, the confidant of Stalin. Moscow did not fail to point out discreetly to Berlin the implications of this change. If the talks made no further progress until July, one reason was Germany's suspicion that Moscow merely intended to use her tractability as a means of exerting pressure in its treaty discussions with the West. But the slow progress of these discussions was to be the very reason why the German-Soviet talks quickly gathered substance from the end of July onwards. On August 12th, the same day that an Anglo-French Staff mission began talks in Moscow about the proposed military convention, the Russians intimated in Berlin that they were ready to open direct discussions on all questions of mutual interest, with Berlin as the suggested meeting-place. Suddenly all obstacles were removed on the German side too. Ribbentrop declared his willingness to come to Moscow and suggested an earlier date. After agreeing on the points to be discussed, Hitler sent a personal telegram to Stalin and so managed to get the date of Ribbentrop's visit advanced several days beyond that suggested by the Russians. Time was running short if he was to attack Poland this year. On August 23rd Ribbentrop flew to Moscow and the same night signed a German-Soviet non-aggression pact with Molotov. But the most important result of the Berlin-Moscow understanding was contained in an additional secret protocol which defined each side's sphere of interest in Europe. In this secret agreement Germany declared her disinterest in Finland, Latvia, Estonia and Bessarabia. "In the event of a territorial and political transformation of the territories belonging to the Polish State," as the protocol so unequivocally put it, the interests of both sides were to be delimited approximately by the line of the Narev, Vistula and San.

For both countries the pact meant a complete reversal of their existing policies. For both it was in blatant contrast to their ideologies: to Nazi anti-Bolshevism as much as to Communist anti-Fascism. The cynicism with which both sides brushed aside ideological obstacles, and the ease with which their propaganda machines managed to bring round the mass of their followers, showed an underlying kinship. Neither Hitler nor Stalin can seriously have believed that the *entente* would last. For each it was a tactical move within the framework of his political ideas, whose final aims were directed implacably against the other party.

Hitler was so obsessed by his Polish plans that in order to avoid the danger of a two-front war — the only obstacle he took seriously — he was prepared to pay the enormous price of the Russian pact and give up vast sectors of the belt of small states which screened Central Europe from the Soviet Union. He was convinced that the Western Powers would sacrifice Poland, which in its position of a wedge between two big Powers was now militarily out of their reach. To gain temporary freedom of action, he played this shortsighted and frivolous game on a plane which was no longer merely German but European, a game which in the end made possible Russia's expansion to Central Germany.

The Russians seemed to have given much more serious thought to the conclusion of their pact with Hitler. Their official argument, that they merely wanted peace, is refuted by the Additional Protocol, which contained the draft for the partition of Poland. The truth is that by making the pact with Hitler, Stalin made the war possible. For a treaty between Russia and the Western Powers would have been the one means — at least at this stage — of preventing Hitler from setting the world alight. But faced with the alternative of a pact with the West or a pact with Hitler, Stalin chose the latter. Hitler had more to offer: a chance for the Soviet Union to extend its influence in the East European states which the Treaty of Versailles had established in Russia's absence as an anti-Soviet *cordon sanitaire*. The pact with the Western Powers would have obliged the Soviet Union to defend these states. If the Russians were convinced that Hitler would sooner or later make war on them, there was a good argument for gaining time and strategic outposts to the West, both of which were offered by the pact with Germany. For the rest, the Russians may have doubted if a treaty with the Western Powers would really mean effective protection against a German attack. Munich was an awkward memory. For there the Western Powers had ignored Russia and come to terms with Germany. After that, it did not seem so very far-fetched to suppose that Britain might one day come to another agreement with Hitler and grant him a free hand in the East. From the Communist point of view, the Western Powers and

Fascist Germany belonged to the same world of capitalist imperialism and shared a common bond of anti-Communist solidarity. It was an old maxim of Communist ideology that the world revolution was furthered most effectively by internecine wars between the capitalist states. This was yet another prospect offered by the pact with Hitler.

When the news of the German-Soviet Pact broke on August 23rd it was a shock to the whole world. War now seemed inevitable, for Hitler no longer saw any obstacle in his way to attacking Poland. The feverish diplomatic activity in the European capitals during the last week of August was no longer capable of deflecting fate. As for Germany, she was mainly concerned to justify her own action and ensure that future debates on the question of guilt would be coloured by the Nazi viewpoint.

On August 22nd the British Government was already apprised of the imminent conclusion of the Moscow Pact. Chamberlain lost no time in assuring Hitler, by a letter on the same evening, that Britain would stand by her obligations to Poland under any circumstances. On August 25th Britain confirmed her attitude by signing a formal pact of assistance with Poland. The change of attitude which Hitler had hoped would result from his pact with Russia did not occur. But while London considered the implications of the pact quite calmly, France was thrown into some confusion. At first Daladier treated the news from Moscow as a journalistic hoax. There were still illusions in France about reaching a Western agreement with Moscow, and the defeatist question "Mourir pour Dantzig?" went the rounds of the country. In Poland the atmosphere was much quieter, for the nation's conceit at its own strength seemed to prevent it from realising that the German-Soviet agreement had put it in mortal danger. An unexpected and highly embarrassing development for Hitler was the reaction of Italy in face of the British stand: on the afternoon of August 25th Mussolini

informed Hitler that Italy, unfortunately, was not ready for war.

Probably under the impact of this news, which reached Berlin simultaneously with the news of the signing of the Anglo-Polish Treaty, Hitler, on the evening of August 25th, revoked the order, given a few hours before, to attack Poland next morning. All at once he seems to have become unsure of himself, if only in the matter of timing. He wanted to gain time for discussion, in the hope that Britain would yet give in.

About noon on the same day he had already made a far-reaching political offer to Henderson, the British Ambassador in Berlin. He may only have intended to confuse London at the moment of the attack on Poland (which, at the time of the meeting with Henderson, was still planned for the next day) and to paralyse its ability to act. But at the same time it was once again an expression of his old dream of Anglo-German friendship. He offered to guarantee the British Empire and make Germany's resources available for its defence. Britain, in return, was to give him a free hand in Poland. London's answer was handed over by Henderson on the evening of August 28th. While making cautious advances regarding a future Anglo-German understanding, it declared a peaceful settlement of the German-Polish conflict to be an indispensable prerequisite, and that this settlement must be reached on the basis of negotiations between equals. It urgently recommended direct negotiations between Germany and Poland.

On the evening of August 29th Hitler gave his answer to the British Ambassador: he was prepared to take up the British suggestion of a German-Polish understanding and would expect a Polish representative with full plenary powers on August 30th. This was a thinly veiled ultimatum, formulated in the knowledge that it would be impossible for Poland to send a qualified representative in so short a time. Hitler had no desire for any such negotiations. Sure enough, Britain declared his demand to be unacceptable in this form. The memory of Hácha's visit to Berlin was still too vivid. During the night of August 30th–31st, Henderson handed a statement of his Government's point of view to the German Foreign Minister. In a scene which has become famous and which hardly has an equal in the history of diplomacy, Ribbentrop told the British Ambassador that further efforts for German-Polish negotiations would be pointless because no Polish representative had appeared. Ribbentrop read out a sixteen-point document containing relatively modest German demands on Poland which he claimed were to have been submitted to the Polish representative but which were now declared ineffective. Against all diplomatic usage, he refused to hand the Ambassador the text of this document.

With this the Anglo-German negotiations reached a stalemate. In the last week of August they had been several times crossed and supplemented by the unofficial Swedish intermediary Dahlerus, who used his connections with Goering to try to bring about an understanding between London and Berlin in the mistaken belief that Hitler might still choose peace. In fact, Berlin had used him as a tool in an attempt to keep England out of a war on which Hitler had already decided.

Late in the afternoon of August 31st Lipski, the Polish Ambassador, appeared after all at the Wilhelmstrasse and said his Government had been notified by the British Government of the possibility of direct negotiations; the Polish Government was glad to accept the suggestion and would send a formal reply within a few hours. Since Lipski could produce no special authority for making immediate decisions, Ribbentrop terminated the conversation in a few minutes. Further talks were indeed pointless. Six hours earlier Hitler had given the final order for the attack on Poland, due to take place early next day. Even a last-minute attempt by Mussolini to arrange a conference of the Great Powers could no longer avert the disaster. When, on September 2nd, Mussolini received the British Government's condition that Hitler must first withdraw his troops from Poland, he did not even pass it on to Berlin. Hitler had made it plain that Italy's attempt at mediation was unwelcome.

In the early hours of September 1st, without declaration of war, Germany attacked Poland. Hitler had ordered the attack knowing that he was risking a world war, although he nourished to the last a hope that Britain would remain neutral or at least passive. On September 3rd, Britain and France, in accordance with their treaty obligations to Poland, declared war on Germany.

HISTORY'S CASE AGAINST HITLER:
A FRENCH VIEW

MAURICE BAUMONT

In the opinion of many scholars, the most distinguished multi-volume history of modern Europe in any language just after World War II was the collection edited by two noted French historians: Louis Halphen and Philippe Sagnac, _Peuples et civilisations_. The period 1918–1939 in that series is treated in two volumes by Maurice Baumont. Between the World Wars Baumont served both the Reparations Commission and the League of Nations. He is author of a study of the fall of the German monarchy in 1918 and other books, and is professor of contemporary history at the Sorbonne. He served as chief French editor on the United States-British-French committee that after 1945 edited captured documents of the German Foreign Ministry for publication. The volume from which this reading is taken was basically written in 1945 and revised in the light of the new German documents.

ON August 22nd [1939], Chamberlain informs Hitler in a personal letter that the Russo-German pact in no way modifies the British attitude with respect to Poland and repeats his conviction that an Anglo-German war would be "the worst catastrophe." He begs him to undertake direct discussion with the Polish government. "It has been maintained," he declares, "that if His Majesty's Government had more clearly defined its position in 1914, the great catastrophe could have been avoided. Whether this statement be justified or not, His Majesty's Government is determined that such a tragic misunderstanding not repeat itself."

During an interview with Ambassador Henderson, Hitler specifically accuses England of playing the champion of inferior races and of seeking the destruction of Germany, whose vital interests cannot any longer be sacrificed. He prefers rather "to declare war at the age of fifty," he adds, than to wait until fifty-five or sixty. "The Germans will fight until the last man," and

will in three weeks overcome the resistance of the Polish army which, with only a mediocre artillery and an insignificant air force, completely lacks anti-tank weapons.

This same August 22nd, Hitler announces to his commanders-in-chief that conflict is inevitable. "I will give some propaganda reason for starting the war: it makes little difference whether or not it's plausible. When one begins a war, what counts is not right, but victory."

On August 23rd, he replies to Chamberlain, pretending that the unconditional assurance of assistance promised to Poland by England has encouraged Polish terrorism "against a million and a half Germans living in Poland"; Germany cannot "tolerate the continuation of such persecution." He lays the blame on "those who, after the crime of Versailles, have always obstinately opposed any peaceful revision" of the treaty. "All my life," he concludes, "I have fought for Anglo-German friendship," and he deplores "the futility of such an endeavour."

From that time on the Germans concen-

From Maurice Baumont, _La faillite de la paix_ (1918–1939), 2 vols., 3rd ed. (Paris, 1951), II, 877–888. Reprinted by permission of the Presses Universitaires de France. Translated by Dr. Rima Reck.

trate on deliberate provocations. Border incidents, carefully prepared, break out. Hitler has given the order to furnish Polish uniforms to the Gestapo. Dead men dressed in Polish uniforms are found on German territory; the victims come from concentration camps. On August 23rd, the Senate of Danzig names Forster *Gauleiter* (district leader), although this office was not mentioned in the free city's constitution. More and more inexorably the inevitability of conflict sharpens.

In vain on August 25th Roosevelt addresses a last plea for amicable settlement to Hitler and to the President of the Polish republic. In vain the Pope, Queen Wilhelmina, and Leopold III try to use their authority with the Führer. In vain Daladier appeals to the "soldier of the last war": "The fate of peace is in your hands alone."

Nevertheless, by this time, the end of August, Hitler has lost his illusions: he no longer counts on the abstention of Great Britain and France. On the contrary, he believes in what he calls "the great struggle." Once Poland has been rapidly crushed, he will direct all his forces against the West. He thinks that war against the Western powers may last a long time. But thanks to the modernity of its weapons, Germany has all the advantages on her side. Sure of Italy, which, while she hasn't a very solid army, brings a sizeable air force and fleet, Germany has nothing to fear from the Franco-British alliance. As for the United States, it does not count from the military point of view. In addition, its neutrality will be solidly maintained by the action of the isolationists, and in 1940 a presidential election will totally paralyze the country.

The Führer is in a hurry to start the campaign, before the roads and airfields are rendered unusable by rain, fog and mud, since during autumn and winter Poland becomes "a great swamp unsuitable for military operations." As soon as the 24th of August, immediately after the signing of the treaty of Moscow, he sets the attack on Poland at August 26th, at dawn. But on

the evening of the 25th, the tragic expiration date is put off. As Hitler declares to General Keitel, he "needs time to negotiate." He still wants to try, in a last effort, to isolate Poland, and to take his chances on seeing the "Czech affair" begin all over, as he explains to Goering. In this case either he would have to deal militarily only with Poland, or he would constrain her to subjection without war. A delay is necessary in order to pursue negotiations with Great Britain which Italy urgently recommends. In addition, two disturbing bits of news, which come to light on this "black day" of the 25th, serve to have the military measures planned for August 26th deferred for the time being: Mussolini declares he cannot fight at the side of Germany, and the Anglo-Polish mutual assistance pact is signed in London.

After Hitler has told Mussolini on August 26th that he is going to commence military operations against Poland, on the very same day and after much hesitation, Il Duce decides to inform him that Italy is not ready to march "for the moment": she needs war materials and raw materials. "At the time of our meetings, the war was planned for a date some time after 1942; at that date, I would have been ready on land, on the sea, and in the air. In view of the present state of Italian preparation for war, I want to let you know in advance, as your faithful friend, that it would be better if I did not take the initiative in the matter of military activities." When Berlin inquires after the Italian needs which should be met, Rome makes enormous demands, enough, said Ciano, to "kill a bull if he could read," and as a final discouragement to the Germans, Ambassador Attolico coldly affirms that the delivery should be immediate. But Hitler is none the less decided on marching; on August 26th he assures Mussolini that he understands his difficulties. He will permit Italy to abstain from entering the war "for the moment." Appealing to his "understanding," he begs him to keep his non-belligerence secret as long as possible and to take military measures designed to immobilize the French forces. Satisfied to "remain at the window" for the moment, Mussolini once again expresses his regrets at not being able to take part.

To sign the mutual assistance pact between Great Britain and Poland two days after the conclusion of the Russo-German pact is a solemn reaffirmation of the British pledge. Hitler wonders if this striking confirmation, which reinforces engagements already taken with respect to Warsaw, has not been brought on by Italy's attitude, which became known immediately to the Foreign Office. Anticipating the psychological effect which his agreement with Moscow will have on the world, he would like to prevent the British from honoring their obligations toward Poland. As "a man of great decisions," he sends for Ambassador Henderson in the early afternoon of the 25th and calmly expresses to him his burning desire to be on good terms with England. Of course, he is absolutely obliged to straighten out "the problems of Danzig and the Corridor"; faced with intolerable provocations, he is determined to put an end to a "Macedonian" situation on his Eastern borders. Nevertheless, he proposes the conclusion of an understanding with the British government as soon as the Polish difference is settled. He "accepts the British Empire"; he is prepared for "a reasonable limitation on armaments"; he demands no modifications of Western borders. He means to make, toward England, a gesture as comprehensive, as decisive as the one he has just carried out with regard to the Soviet Union. But the United Kingdom must keep out of a war in which, he specifies, "contrary to the last war, the Reich would not be obliged to fight on two fronts," and he insists on his "irrevocable decision never again to go to war with Russia." He wants the British government to persuade Poland "not to be unreasonable." "An artist and not a politician by nature," he would like to end his days devoted to works of peace, "after the settlement of the Polish question." He suggests that Henderson fly to London immediately to inform the British government personally.

On this same afternoon of August 25th, trying up to the last minute to disunite the Allies, Hitler calls the ambassador of France, Coulondre, and begs him to convey to Daladier his assurance that he has renounced any claims to Alsace-Lorraine and that he would find it very painful to be dragged into a war with France because of Poland: "the blood of two equally brave nations will be spilled." But he can no longer endure the massacre of Germans by the Poles and he will reply "with force" to any new provocations.

On August 26th, Henderson reaches London with a "*note verbale*" which had been given to him the evening before and of which Hitler said to Ribbentrop: "Let us send this note to the English in any case, and if they react, we shall see."

The days of the 27th and the 28th pass in waiting for a reply to what the Führer called "his last proposition." During the night of August 28th, Henderson comes bringing this reply to Hitler. Firm and sharp, the British reply suggests the resolution of the Polish dispute by means of direct negotiations between Germany and Poland. Moved by a conciliating mildness, Hitler does not reject this offer. While he declares his demand for the abandonment of Danzig and the Corridor, as well as a rectification of the border of Upper Silesia, he states himself ready to make one more gesture toward a peaceful solution and promises he will reply to the British note on the next day. Following the example of England, Mussolini strongly advises him to "follow the road of negotiations." During the evening of the 29th, while proclaiming that he is "sceptical about the chances of success," Hitler informs Henderson that he accepts the British proposal of direct discussions with Poland: he is prepared to receive a Polish plenipotentiary. In answer to the British note, the German note declares that fair and equitable proposals for the solution of the Danzig and Corridor questions will be remitted to a Polish plenipotentiary if one presents himself in Berlin before midnight on August 30th. Henderson points out that to demand the arrival of this agent by the next day "resembles an ultimatum"; but Hitler and Ribbentrop do not admit this; they both insist that they wish "only to insist on the urgency of the circumstances, when two fully mobilized armies stand face to face."

Henderson invites Polish Ambassador Lipski to urgently entreat his government to send someone to Berlin without delay. Under pressure from Chamberlain and Ambassador Henderson, a direct conversation seems on the point of being begun between Germany and Poland. It appears that the high point of the crisis is past and that, at the last moment, a peaceful solution is in sight.

But the Poles no longer have any confidence in the Führer's word: how can they have faith in his promises? They remember the fate of Schuschnigg and Hácha. As a British magistrate will state it at the Nuremberg trials, they don't want "lightheartedly to toss a fly into this spider's web." Already Colonel Beck is disturbed at the idea that the British should express a definitive opinion on Polish matters without consulting him. He refuses to send to Berlin a plenipotentiary charged with receiving German proposals. On August 30th the British ambassador to Warsaw reports that the Poles "would fight and die rather than submit to such a humiliation": they would like to negotiate in Italy or in a neutral country. That evening Halifax himself telegraphs Henderson that he considers the procedure indicated by the Germans "unreasonable"; to it he prefers "the normal procedure" of diplomatic relations.

On August 30th, in Berlin, they wait in vain for the Polish plenipotentiary. The hours pass and no one comes to receive the memorandum with sixteen points prepared by Hitler himself. The news of general mobilization decreed in Poland shows that the course of events can no longer be modified; the white placards have appeared on the walls of Warsaw late that morning.

Germany, which has carefully avoided giving her mobilization an official character, cries provocation. Things become irremediably worse. All hope is disappearing.

Late that evening, Ambassador Henderson requests a meeting with Ribbentrop. At midnight, Henderson informs the minister that if the German government is willing to submit its proposals with respect to Poland to him, the British government is prepared to use its influence in Warsaw in order to arrive at a solution. Ribbentrop, who will claim at Nuremberg that the Führer ordered him to communicate only the substance of his proposals, reads the whole German note to Henderson, but very quickly. During this disagreeable interview, where he displays an attitude which is "merely an imitation of Hitler in his worst moments," Ribbentrop refuses to remit a copy of the document in which are defined the demands. Nervous and violent, he declares that, in any case, it is too late, since no Polish plenipotentiary has arrived in Berlin. It is no longer a question of German proposals; they have lapsed at the very moment when they were formulated, and Ribbentrop shouts that British mediation has had "only one result": the general mobilization decreed in Poland.

On August 31st, at 2 o'clock in the morning, Henderson summarizes for Lipski the demands of the German government: the return of Danzig to Germany; a plebiscite for the Corridor within a year, with Gdynia remaining Polish, in any case; an extra-territorial transit zone for the side which does not get the majority; the possibility of a transfer of Poles to Poland if the majority opts for Germany; the eventual exchange of minority populations. Henderson adds that at first glance these proposals do not seem to him "too unreasonable, as a whole." In fact, they attenuate to some extent the National Socialist wishes; for, as Hitler will himself confess, they are designed to give the German people proof that everything was done to preserve peace. Nevertheless, these proposals which, compared to the frenzy of

Nazi propaganda, seem almost moderate, had no chance at all of being accepted. As Léon Noël, then French ambassador to Warsaw, wrote, "There was no chance at the end of August, 1939, not the slightest, that in order to avoid war, Poland would resign herself to accept the reincorporation of Danzig with Germany; or agree that the fate of the Corridor be determined by a plebiscite in which former German functionaries who had left the country in 1918, their wives and the children born there, take part . . . ; or that the government of Warsaw allow the measures aimed at the Germans of Poland since the reconstitution of the Republic to be called in question again . . . , or consent to endow this minority with a statute which in the end would have placed Poland under a veritable German protectorate."

Lipski, whom Henderson has advised to establish direct contact with the German government, sends Prince Lubomirski by auto to Poznań, from which he flies on to Warsaw. On August 31st, reprimanded by the ambassadors of France and Great Britain, Beck declares that he is prepared to enter into negotiations with the German government and that he charges Ambassador Lipski to make inquiries at the Wilhelmstrasse; but he does not authorize him to accept any proposals on his own and he adds that, should he find it necessary to go to Berlin, he does not intend to be treated there as was Hácha.

The confusion of these nightmarish days is heightened by the interventions of Goering, which only came to light five [sic; six] years later, at the time of the Nuremberg trials. Official negotiations of very great importance are being conducted between Berlin and London, unknown to Warsaw, and also unknown to the French government itself, which was, Chamberlain wrote, incapable of "keeping a secret more than half an hour." This feverish activity does not seem to have greatly influenced the course of events.

While Himmler is pushing for aggression against Poland and while Ribbentrop,

confident of the gigantic power of Germany, is passively abandoning himself to the brutal politics which the Führer passionately prefers without any attempt at a compromise, the "Marshal of the Reich," Goering, is fundamentally of Il Duce's opinion: he does not want war at this moment. Henderson is convinced that his personal desire for peace and for good relations with England is sincere. Goering has recourse to the services of a Swedish friend, the engineer Dahlerus, in order to make contact with some eminent personalities in England: he wants to give the British various possibilities so that they will not make good the guarantees given to Poland, or so that they will force her to be more docile, in order to arrive, to use his phrase, at "a peaceful solution" similar to that of Munich. In July and August, particularly from the 25th to the 30th, Dahlerus goes back and forth in a special plane between Berlin and London, where very frequently he sees the highest personages of the two governments, including Hitler, Chamberlain, and Halifax.

On the night of the 26th or 27th of August, highly agitated, Hitler is railing against England, before Dahlerus. He cries that in order to annihilate his enemies he will build planes and submarines, "submarines and still more submarines." "At each word," recounts Dahlerus, "he raised his voice as if he were addressing a huge audience. Gathering his strength, he screamed, 'I will build planes, planes, and still more planes.' He looked like a phantom out of a history book." However, in spite of his violence, Hitler proposes an agreement or alliance with Great Britain, which he swears to defend against any attack with the German army. In return, Great Britain must support him in the annexation of Danzig and the Corridor. He no longer speaks simply of "rights to the Corridor," he wants the Corridor. Chamberlain will express his surprise over this. It is true that in his offer, which he calls "magnanimous," the Führer swears to safeguard the new borders of Poland, provided that the German minorities receive sufficient guarantees. Finally, he suggests an arrangement concerning the former German colonies.

The British examine each of these points "with great care." They refuse to discuss the question of the colonies before Germany has demobilized. They demand that the Polish borders be guaranteed jointly by Germany, the Soviet Union, Italy, France, and England. As for the Corridor, they propose immediate negotiations with Poland. They accept the conclusion of an agreement with Germany, while declining the offer to defend the British Empire.

Hitler approves of the British point of view, so that Goering, on the morning of August 29th, declares that peace is assured. On August 30th, Dahlerus is again in London, where it is suspected that Germany is trying to provoke a rupture between England and Poland by these manoeuvres; he sees Chamberlain, Halifax, Sir Horace Wilson. . . . He is told that one should not wait until Warsaw sends envoys to Berlin in order to negotiate; Hitler, consulted by telephone, demands that the meeting take place in Berlin. Dahlerus leaves again for Germany, where, on the evening of the 30th or 31st of August, he sees Goering, and on the morning of the 31st, Henderson. Having received the text of the German proposals which Ribbentrop refused him, the ambassador of England communicates it to Lipski. He sends Dahlerus himself, accompanied by a British diplomat, to the Polish ambassador. Very nervous, Lipski declares that in case of war, the Poles will march on Berlin; having lived in Germany for five years now, he is convinced that revolution will break out there; but if Poland is abandoned by her allies, she will fight alone.

Meanwhile British diplomacy, increasing friendly contacts with Rome, has appealed to Il Duce to undertake peacemaking action. On the morning of August 31st, Ciano suggests to Halifax that Danzig be turned over to Germany in order to rally her to the idea of an international confer-

ence. The British minister replies that such a proposal is unacceptable. The idea of a conference is clarified in the course of an interview with the French ambassador to Rome, François-Poncet. During the afternoon, Mussolini offers Hitler his mediation; in the evening, Hitler rejects this offer "in order not to place him in a disagreeable situation." In the early afternoon of the 31st, enlarging the debate, Ciano proposes from his side to call together for September 5th an international conference designed to revise the clauses of the Treaty of Versailles which are causing the trouble in Europe. He will address an invitation to Germany only if France and Great Britain approve of his project. It appears that he is going to obtain the agreement of Paris, where the Minister of Foreign Affairs, Georges Bonnet, accused of being evasive, is willing to do the impossible to save the peace, in spite of the split in the cabinet during the evening. Ciano seems also about to obtain the acquiescence of London, although the Italian proposal arouses strong distrust there.

Finally, before declaring themselves, France and England wish to know the outcome of the Polish-German negotiations.

On that same day of August 31st, Halifax has begged Ciano to intervene in order finally to establish a direct contact in Berlin between the Germans and the Poles. Ribbentrop agrees to receive Ambassador Lipski that evening. The latter has asked for an interview early that afternoon and declares that the Polish government "looks with favor" on the British suggestions aimed at a direct conversation; but he himself is not authorized to accept any conditions and has no power to negotiate.

Hitler seizes this pretext to break off, and immediately issues the order fixing the beginning of the attack on Poland at dawn, September 1st: he thinks the moment is favorable and he strikes. At 10:00 p.m., the German radio makes public the proposals "for the settlement of the problems of Danzig, the Corridor, etc.," which the German government wished to present to a Polish plenipotentiary who did not arrive. The Germans have deciphered a telegram transmitting the Polish government's instructions to Lipski: "avoid conducting official negotiations, no matter what the circumstances." Goering has this information get to London by way of Dahlerus, although it reveals that Berlin knows the Polish code.

At 4:45 A.M., September 1st, the German army enters Poland, after the Supreme Soviet in Moscow has ratified, the previous evening, the Russo-German Pact. Hitler, whom Dahlerus sees during the day, "no longer has any control over himself"; he cries out, "We will fight ten years if necessary," beating his fist "with such violence that he almost falls down."

General mobilization is ordered in England and in France, and the governments of these two countries inform Germany that evening that they will stand behind their obligations to Poland, if German forces are not immediately removed from Polish territory. Are the roads to peace definitely closed?

The British government, henceforth abandoning any idea of conciliation, judges that German aggression makes impossible the conference suggested by Italy, while Paris, which is far less firm than London, sends a favorable reply to Rome at the entreaty of Georges Bonnet and insists that Il Duce sound out Berlin on the subject. This time, Hitler does not at once reject the proposal. Agreeing that Poland, too, be invited, according to the desire expressed by the Quai d'Orsay, Count Ciano begs the French government to insist to Colonel Beck on an immediate acceptance. But the Colonel no longer wishes, "in open war," to hear talk of a conference; he declares that he is interested only in "the common action" which the Allies must undertake with absolute firmness in order to resist aggression.

During the morning of September 1st Forster, *Gauleiter* of Danzig, proclaims its reincorporation in the Reich, and this reincorporation is immediately confirmed by the Reichstag. That afternoon, Italy proclaims her "non-belligerence." While the servile Tiso is calling for German aid for Slovakia, "threatened by Poland," on the afternoon of September 2nd Ciano is still proposing by telephone to Georges Bonnet and Lord Halifax the immediate meeting of an international conference of five at San Remo, preceded by an armistice. Without refusing, and in spite of the efforts of Georges Bonnet, England still clings up to the last moment to a vain hope of compromise; she lays down the evacuation of Polish territory occupied by the Germans as a preliminary condition. The last glimmer of peace is extinguished. There will be no "new Munich conference" at San Remo.

On September 2nd, Halifax urges Paris to make a decision. Daladier addresses the Chamber of Deputies that afternoon to ask for a vote of confidence. Bonnet temporizes in a manner which very much worries the Poles. He would like to prolong the delay by forty-eight hours, at the end of which in case Germany refuses to receive the communiqués from Great Britain and France, the latter would have the right to open hostilities. To Lord Halifax he stresses "the very great responsibility" which England assumes toward France, at a time when "the evacuation of women and children from the large cities" is not complete and when bombing aircraft are not prepared to step in. In London, the opposition is getting impatient over the government, which is accountable for British honor, being compromised by French hesitation. The French ambassador to London, Corbin, is assailed by strong imprecations. That evening, Halifax telephones to Bonnet that the declaration of war will be issued publicly the next morning: Bonnet refuses to commit himself to a parallel decision.

On the night of September 2nd or 3rd, the Italian ambassador to Paris telephones Ciano to ask him, on behalf of Georges Bonnet, if it would not be possible to obtain at least "a symbolic retreat of German forces from Poland." Ciano immediately turns aside the proposal, which proves, he notes, that "France anticipates the great struggle without enthusiasm and full of uncertainty."

On Sunday, September 3rd, with the authorization of Hitler, Goering declares that he is ready to leave immediately for London. Dahlerus, who telephones the Foreign Office, is told that this proposal cannot be considered before a written reply to the British communiqué has been made. Dahlerus will conclude that, to his great disappointment, he realized that the aim of the Germans had been "to separate Poland and Great Britain, and with the consent of Great Britain to occupy Poland without running the risk of a war with Great Britain and France."

September 3rd, at 5:00 A.M., the British ambassador to Berlin is asked by London to demand an interview with the Minister of Foreign Affairs for 9:00 A.M. He submits a last note to the German government: if Germany does not declare herself disposed to reply to the British communiqué of September 1st within two hours, a state of war will be declared between the two countries. At noon, the French ambassador informs the Wilhelmstrasse that "the French government finds itself . . . obliged to fulfill, beginning today, September 3rd, at 5:00 P.M., her obligations toward Poland, which are known to the German government." Thus England, at 11:00 A.M., and France, at 5:00 P.M., go to war with Germany.

A CHALLENGE TO NUREMBERG AND POSTWAR HISTORY

A. J. P. TAYLOR

The previous three readings emphasize German responsibility for the outbreak of the Second World War. Here is an attack on that "orthodox" interpretation. The author, A. J. P. Taylor, is Fellow of Magdalen College, Oxford University. In books on nineteenth-century Italy, Imperial Germany's acquisition of colonies in the 1880's, Bismarck, the course of German history, the Hapsburg monarchy, and diplomatic history, Taylor had made himself known before 1961 for his research, his vivid and sometimes shocking interpretations, and his terse and ironical style, drawing heavily upon cynicism and paradox. It was usually said of Taylor's works, even before 1961, that they were "thought provoking," which they were. Many historians also considered their interpretations perverse or irresponsible. This reading is taken from a book of 1961 that stirred more controversy than any of Taylor's other works. It is inaccurate to say simply that the book is "pro-German" or "pro-Hitler." In his early pages Taylor briefly seems to imply that Germany should have been dismembered into separate states in 1919; that a Germany left united, as if by some kind of geopolitical natural law, inevitably would reassert the power it had briefly established with the surrender of Soviet Russia at Brest-Litovsk early in 1918. Taylor, who in the Chamberlain era opposed appeasement of Nazi Germany, in his 1961 treatment frequently justifies Hitler's demands and criticizes British policy for not appeasing Hitler more fully. But he is not consistent in his argument. Would Taylor's interpretation have been different if he had made use of the records of the International Military Tribunal, which he criticized as historical sources and failed to mention in his bibliography?

THE leading authors to whom we turn for accounts of the origins of the second World war — Namier, Wheeler-Bennett, Wiskemann in English, Baumont in French — all published their books soon after the war ended; and all expressed views which they had held while the war was on, or even before it began. Twenty years after the outbreak of the first World war, very few people would have accepted without modification the explanations for it given in August 1914. Twenty years and more after the outbreak of the second World war nearly everyone accepts the explanations which were given in September 1939. . . .

If the evidence had been sufficiently conflicting, scholars would soon have been found to dispute the popular verdict, however generally accepted. This has not happened; and for two apparently contradictory reasons — there is at once too much evidence and too little. The evidence of which there is too much is that collected for the trials of war-criminals in Nuremberg.

From *The Origins of the Second World War* by A. J. P. Taylor, pp. 9, 13–14, 71–72, 131–132, 195–196, 209–211, 215–216, 218–220, 250, 263–264, 268–269, 272–278. Copyright © 1961 by A. J. P. Taylor. Reprinted by permission of Atheneum Publishers, New York, and Hamish Hamilton, Ltd., London.

Though these documents look imposing in their endless volumes, they are dangerous material for a historian to use. They were collected, hastily and almost at random, as a basis for lawyers' briefs. This is not how historians would proceed. The lawyer aims to make a case; the historian wishes to understand a situation. The evidence which convinces lawyers often fails to satisfy us; our methods seem singularly imprecise to them. But even lawyers must now have qualms about the evidence at Nuremberg. The documents were chosen not only to demonstrate the war-guilt of the men on trial, but to conceal that of the prosecuting Powers. If any of the four Powers who set up the Nuremberg tribunal had been running the affair alone, it would have thrown the mud more widely. The Western Powers would have brought in the Nazi-Soviet Pact; the Soviet Union would have retaliated with the Munich conference and more obscure transactions. Given the four-Power tribunal, the only possible course was to assume the sole guilt of Germany in advance. The verdict preceded the tribunal; and the documents were brought in to sustain a conclusion which had already been settled. Of course the documents are genuine. But they are "loaded"; and anyone who relies on them finds it almost impossible to escape from the load with which they are charged.

If we seek instead for evidence assembled in a more detached and scholarly way, we discover how much worse off we are than our predecessors who studied the origins of the first World war. . . .

In principle and doctrine, Hitler was no more wicked and unscrupulous than many other contemporary statesmen. In wicked acts he outdid them all. The policy of Western statesmen also rested ultimately on force — French policy on the army, British policy on sea-power. But these statesmen hoped that it would not be necessary to use this force. Hitler intended to use his force, or would at any rate threaten to use it. If Western morality seemed superior, this was largely because it was the morality of the

status quo; Hitler's was the immorality of revision. There was a curious, though only superficial, contradiction in Hitler between aims and methods. His aim was change, the overthrow of the existing European order; his method was patience. Despite his bluster and violent talk, he was a master in the game of waiting. He never made a frontal attack on a prepared position — at least never until his judgement had been corrupted by easy victories. Like Joshua before the walls of Jericho, he preferred to wait until the forces opposing him had been sapped by their own confusions and themselves forced success upon him. He had already applied this method to gain power in Germany. He did not "seize" power. He waited for it to be thrust upon him by the men who had previously tried to keep him out. In January 1933 Papen and Hindenburg were imploring him to become Chancellor; and he graciously consented. So it was to be in foreign affairs. Hitler did not make precise demands. He announced that he was dissatisfied; and then waited for the concessions to pour into his lap, merely holding out his hand for more. Hitler did not know any foreign countries at first hand. He rarely listened to his foreign minister, and never read the reports of his ambassadors. He judged foreign statesmen by intuition. He was convinced that he had taken the measure of all *bourgeois* politicians, German and foreign alike, and that their nerve would crumble before his did. This conviction was near enough to the truth to bring Europe within sight of disaster. . . .

The watershed between the two World wars extended over precisely two years. Post-war ended when Germany reoccupied the Rhineland on 7 March 1936; pre-war began when she annexed Austria on 13 March 1938. From that moment, change and upheaval went on almost without interruption until the representatives of the Powers, victorious in the second World war, met at Potsdam in July 1945. Who first raised the storm and launched the march of events? The accepted answer is clear: it was Hitler. The moment of his doing so is also accepted: it was on 5 November 1937. We have a record of the statements which he made that day. It is called "the Hossbach memorandum," after the man who made it. This record is supposed to reveal Hitler's plans. Much play was made with it at Nuremberg; and the editors of the *Documents on German Foreign Policy* say that "it provides a summary of German foreign policy in 1937–38." It is therefore worth looking at in detail. Perhaps we shall find in it the explanation of the second World war; or perhaps we shall find only the source of a legend.

That afternoon Hitler called a conference at the Chancellery. It was attended by Blomberg, the minister of war; Neurath, the foreign minister; Fritsch, commander-in-chief of the army; Raeder, commander-in-chief of the navy; and Goering, commander-in-chief of the air force. Hitler did most of the talking. He began with a general disquisition on Germany's need for *Lebensraum*. He did not specify where this was to be found — probably in Europe, though he also discussed colonial gains. But gains there must be. "Germany had to reckon with two hate-inspired antagonists, Britain and France. . . . Germany's problem could only be solved by means of force and this was never without attendant risk." When and how was there to be this resort to force? Hitler discussed three "cases." The first "case" was "period 1943–1945." After that the situation could only change for the worse; 1943 must be the moment for action. Case 2 was civil war in France; if that happened, "the time for action against the Czechs had come." Case 3 was war between France and Italy. This might well occur in 1938; then "our objective must be to overthrow Czechoslovakia and Austria simultaneously." None of these "cases" came true; clearly therefore they do not provide the blueprint for German policy. Nor did Hitler dwell on them. He went on to demonstrate that Germany would gain her aims without a great war; "force" apparently meant to him the threat

of war, not necessarily war itself. The Western Powers would be too hampered and too timid to intervene. "Britain almost certainly, and probably France as well, had written off the Czechs and were reconciled to the fact that this question of Germany would be cleared up in due course." No other Power would intervene. "Poland — with Russia in her rear — will have little inclination to engage in war against a victorious Germany." Russia would be held in check by Japan.

Hitler's exposition was in large part daydreaming, unrelated to what followed in real life. Even if seriously meant, it was not a call to action, at any rate not to the action of a great war; it was a demonstration that a great war would not be necessary. Despite the preliminary talk about 1943–1945, its solid core was the examination of the chances for peaceful triumphs in 1938, when France would be preoccupied elsewhere. Hitler's listeners remained doubtful. The generals insisted that the French army would be superior to the German even if engaged against Italy as well. Neurath doubted whether a Mediterranean conflict between France and Italy were imminent. Hitler waved these doubts aside: "he was convinced of Britain's non-participation, and therefore he did not believe in the probability of belligerent action by France against Germany." There is only one safe conclusion to be drawn from this rambling disquisition: Hitler was gambling on some twist of fortune which would present him with success in foreign affairs, just as a miracle had made him Chancellor in 1933. There was here no concrete plan, no directive for German policy in 1937 and 1938. Or if there were a directive, it was to wait upon events. . . .

The losses of territory to Poland were, for most Germans, the indelible grievance against Versailles. Hitler undertook a daring operation over this grievance when he planned cooperation with Poland. But there was a way out. The actual Germans under Polish rule might be forgotten — or withdrawn; what could not be forgiven was the "Polish corridor" which divided East Prussia from the Reich. Here, too, there was a possible compromise. Germany might be satisfied with a corridor across the corridor—a complicated idea for which there were however many precedents in German history. German feeling could be appeased by the recovery of Danzig. This seemed easy. Danzig was not part of Poland. It was a Free City, with its own autonomous administration under a High Commissioner, appointed by the League of Nations. The Poles themselves, in their false pride as a Great Power, had taken the lead in challenging the League's authority. Surely, therefore, they would not object if Germany took the League's place. Moreover, the problem had changed since 1919. Then the port of Danzig had been essential to Poland. Now, with the creation of Gdynia by the Poles, Danzig needed Poland more than the Poles needed Danzig. It should then be easy to arrange for the safeguarding of Poland's economic interests, and yet to recover Danzig for the Reich. The stumbling block would be removed; Germany and Poland could act together in the Ukraine.

On 24 October [1938] Ribbentrop first aired these proposals to Lipski, the Polish ambassador. If Danzig and the Corridor were settled, there could then be "a joint policy towards Russia on the basis of the Anti-Comintern Pact." Hitler was even franker when Beck, the Polish foreign minister, visited him in January 1939: "The divisions which Poland stationed on the Russian frontier saved Germany just so much military expenditure." Of course, he added, "Danzig is German, will always remain German, and will sooner or later become part of Germany." If the question of Danzig were settled, he would be ready to guarantee the Corridor to Poland. Hitler may have been cheating the Poles over Danzig all along—demanding its return as the preliminary to their destruction. But Polish ambitions in the Ukraine were of long standing; Danzig seemed a triviality in comparison. Beck "made no secret of the

fact that Poland had aspirations directed towards the Soviet Ukraine," when Ribbentrop visited Warsaw on 1 February.

Nevertheless, the Poles did not respond to Hitler's offer. Blindly confident in their own strength and contemptuous of Czech softness, they were determined not to yield an inch; this, they believed, was the only safe method of doing business with Hitler. Moreover—a point which Hitler never understood—though they would not cooperate with Soviet Russia against Germany, they were almost equally resolved not to cooperate with Germany against Soviet Russia. They regarded themselves as an independent Great Power; and forgot that they had gained their independence in 1918 only because both Russia and Germany had been defeated. Now they had to choose between Germany and Russia. They chose neither. Only Danzig prevented cooperation between Germany and Poland. For this reason, Hitler wanted to get it out of the way. For precisely the same reason, Beck kept it in the way. It did not cross his mind that this might cause a fatal breach. . . .

On 21 March Lipski called on Ribbentrop and protested against the German behaviour over Slovakia—it "could only be regarded as a blow against Poland." Ribbentrop was in a weak position; and he knew it. To protect himself, he paraded grievances in his turn. Polish newspapers, he complained, were behaving badly: "a gradual stiffening in German Polish relations was becoming apparent." Danzig must return to the Reich—this would rivet Poland to the German side. Then there could be a German guarantee for the Corridor, a non-aggression treaty for 25 years, and "a common policy" in the Ukraine. Lipski was sent off to place this offer before Beck. Cooperation with Poland was still the German aim; Danzig merely the security for it. Hitler himself thought this. On 25 March he issued a directive:

The Führer *does not* wish to solve the Danzig question by force. He does not wish to drive Poland into the arms of Britain by this.

A possible military occupation of Danzig could be contemplated *only* if L[ipski] gave an indication that the Polish Government could not justify voluntary cession of Danzig to their own people and that a *fait accompli* would make a solution easier to them.

Hitler's objective was alliance with Poland, not her destruction. Danzig was a tiresome preliminary to be got out of the way. As before, Beck kept it in the way. So long as Danzig stood between Poland and Germany, he could evade the embarrassing offer of a German alliance, and so, as he thought, preserve Polish independence.

Beck's calculations worked, though not precisely as he intended. On 26 March Lipski returned to Berlin. He brought with him a firm refusal to yield over Danzig, though not a refusal to negotiate. Until this moment everything had gone on in secret, with no public hint of German-Polish estrangement. Now it blazed into the open. Beck, to show his resolve, called up Polish reservists. Hitler, to ease things along as he supposed, allowed the German press to write, for the first time, about the German minority in Poland. There were rumours of German troop-movements towards the Polish frontier, just as there had been similar rumours of German movements against Czechoslovakia on 21 May 1938. These new rumours were equally without foundation. They seem to have been started by the Poles. They were however aided on their way by some German generals who claimed to be opponents of Hitler. These generals "warned" the British government. With what object? So that Great Britain would deter Hitler by threatening him with war? Or so that she would cheat him of his war by making the Poles yield over Danzig? Perhaps it was a combination of the two, with an inclination towards the second. At any rate, these generals briefed the correspondent of the *News Chronicle* who was just being expelled from Germany; and on 29 March he, in turn, sounded the alarm at the foreign office. He found willing listeners. After

the occupation of Prague and the supposed threat to Rumania, the British were ready to believe anything. They did not give a thought to Danzig. They supposed that Poland herself was in imminent danger, and likely to succumb. No alarm, it is true, came from the British ambassador in Berlin. But the foreign office had been misled by him on previous occasions, or so it thought; now it preferred the reports of journalists. Immediate action seemed necessary if Polish nerve were to be strengthened and the "peace front" saved.

On 30 March Chamberlain drafted with his own hand an assurance to the Polish government:

If . . . . any action were taken which clearly threatened their independence, and which the Polish Government accordingly felt obliged to resist with their national forces, His Majesty's Government and the French Government would at once lend them all the support in their power.

That afternoon Beck was discussing with the British ambassador how to implement his proposal of a week earlier for a general declaration, when a telegram from London was brought in. The ambassador read out Chamberlain's assurance. Beck accepted it "between two flicks of the ash off his cigarette." Two flicks; and British grenadiers would die for Danzig. Two flicks; and the illusory great Poland, created in 1919, signed her death-warrant. The assurance was unconditional: the Poles alone were to judge whether it should be called upon. . . . British policy had, without design, made Danzig the decisive question for 1939, just as, with more deliberation, it presented the Sudeten Germans as the decisive question in 1938. But with this difference. The Sudeten German question was asked of the Czechs and the French. It was they who were pressed to make concessions, or to face the risk of war. In 1939 the British were themselves at question, faced with the choice between resistance or conciliation. British ministers preferred the second course. They were still the men of peace who had rejoiced at the settlement of Munich. They still hated the prospect of war; still hoped to find a way out by means of negotiation. Moreover, with mounting Japanese pressure in the Far East, they had increasing desire to turn their backs on Europe. Besides, in taking a stand over Danzig they were on peculiarly weak ground. Danzig was the most justified of German grievances; a city of exclusively German population which manifestly wished to return to the Reich and which Hitler himself restrained only with difficulty. The solution, too, seemed peculiarly easy. Halifax never wearied of suggesting that Danzig should return to German sovereignty, with safeguards for Polish trade.

Hitler wanted this also. The destruction of Poland had been no part of his original project. On the contrary, he had wished to solve the question of Danzig so that Germany and Poland could remain on good terms. Was Polish obstinacy then the only thing which stood between Europe and a peaceful outcome? By no means. Previously Danzig might have been settled without implying any upheaval in international relations. Now it had become the symbol of Polish independence; and, with the Anglo-Polish alliance, of British independence as well. Hitler no longer wished merely to fulfill German national aspirations or to satisfy the inhabitants of Danzig. He aimed to show that he had imposed his will on the British and on the Poles. They, on their side, had to deny him this demonstration. All parties aimed at a settlement by negotiation, but only after victory in a war of nerves. There is, of course, an alternative explanation. Some, or all, of the parties may have been driving deliberately for war. There can hardly be any who believe this of Poland; few, even in Germany, who now believe that the British were planning the "encirclement" of Germany in order to impose again the "slavery" of Versailles. Many however believe that Hitler was a modern Attila, loving destruction for its own sake and therefore bent on war

without thought of policy. There is no arguing with such dogmas. Hitler was an extraordinary man; and they may well be true. But his policy is capable of rational explanation; and it is on these that history is built. The escape into irrationality is no doubt easier. The blame for war can be put on Hitler's Nihilism instead of on the faults and failures of European statesmen — faults and failures which their public shared. Human blunders, however, usually do more to shape history than human wickedness. At any rate, this is a rival dogma which is worth developing, if only as an academic exercise. . . .

The economic advance of Soviet Russia, on the other hand, obsessed Hitler. It was indeed startling. During the ten years between 1929 and 1939, while the manufacturing production of Germany increased by 27 per cent and that of Great Britain by 17 per cent, Soviet Russia's increased by 400 per cent; and the process was only beginning. By 1938 Soviet Russia was the second industrial Power in the world, ranking only after the United States. She had still far to go: her population was still impoverished, her resources were hardly tapped. But Germany had not much time if she were to escape being overshadowed, and still less if she hoped to seize the Soviet Ukraine. Here again, it would have made sense for Hitler to plan a great war against Soviet Russia. But, though he often talked of such a war, he did not plan it. German armaments were not designed for such a war. Hitler's rearmament in width was only intended to reinforce a diplomatic war of nerves. Even the rearmament in depth which the German generals wanted would only have equipped Germany for a long-drawn-out war of exhaustion on the Western front such as was fought during the first World war. The Germans had to improvise furiously when they went to war against Soviet Russia in June 1941; and they failed to achieve a quick decisive victory there largely because they had altogether neglected to prepare transport for a war of this nature. In the end, it is hard to tell whether Hitler took the project of war against Soviet Russia seriously; or whether it was an attractive illusion with which he hoped to mesmerise Western statesmen. If he took it seriously, this makes the actual war of 1939 — not a war against Soviet Russia, but a war against the Western Powers, with Germany and Soviet Russia halfway towards an alliance — more inexplicable than ever. Or rather the old, simple explanation reasserts itself. The war of 1939, far from being premeditated, was a mistake, the result on both sides of diplomatic blunders.

Hitler contributed little to the course of diplomacy between April and August 1939. As on previous occasions, he was content to prepare and to wait, confident that the obstacles would somehow disintegrate before him. The example of the Czech crisis was always in his mind. There he had been faced with a strong Czech army and an apparently firm alliance between France and Czechoslovakia. In the end the French gave way, and the Czechs also. It would be the same over Poland. He said of the Western statesmen: "Our opponents are poor creatures [little worms]. I saw them at Munich." He no longer troubled himself about the French. He knew that they would go wherever the British led them, though acting as a brake on the road to war. This time the British would have to decide more directly; and he expected them to decide for concession. Did he also expect the Poles to give way without war? This is harder to answer. On 3 April the armed forces were told to be ready to attack Poland at any time after 1 September, together with an assurance that this would happen only if Poland were isolated — an assurance which Hitler repeated in rather wilder form on 23 May. But these preparations were necessary whether Hitler planned to get his way by war or by threats. They tell us nothing of his real intentions; and probably he had not settled them himself. The war of nerves was enough to be going on with. Here Hitler laid down his challenge clearly. On 28 April he repudiated both the non-aggression Pact with Poland of 1934 and the Anglo-German Naval Agreement of 1935. On the same day he addressed the Reichstag. He recited his offers to Poland, and denounced Polish provocation: the Germans wished to settle the question of Danzig by free negotiation, the Poles answered by relying on force. He was ready to make a new agreement, but only if the Poles changed their attitude — that is, if they gave way over Danzig and abandoned their alliance with Great Britain. He spoke of the British in very different terms: praised the British Empire as "an inestimable factor of value for the whole of human economic and cultural life"; rejected the idea of destroying it as "nothing but the effluence of human wanton destructiveness"; and looked forward warmly to a new agreement when the British had come to their senses. Here, too, the price was the same: concession over Danzig and abandonment of the alliance with Poland. Having thus stated his terms, Hitler withdrew into silence. He was beyond the reach of ambassadors, Ribbentrop almost as much so. There were no further diplomatic exchanges with Poland before the outbreak of war, and none directly with Great Britain until the middle of August.

Decision therefore rested with the British; or rather it was dictated to them by the Anglo-Polish alliance. . . .

Hitler's later behaviour suggests that he had not made up his mind as decisively as he indicated on 23 May. To the very last minute he was battering away for the Polish offer which never came. Maybe he did not expect the Polish nerve to break of itself; but he expected the Western Powers to do the breaking for him, as they had done predominantly with Beneš in 1938. He did not foresee exactly how the nerve of the Western Powers would crumble or precisely what effect this would have on the Poles. Nor was it of much moment to him whether the Poles then gave way without war or were left to be destroyed in isolation; the result would be much the same either way. On the larger point — the crumbling of Western nerve — he never doubted. There are also indications that, as the summer wore on, he began to foresee how this would come about. A collapse of the Anglo-Franco-Soviet negotiations would, he thought, do the trick. . . .

However one spins the crystal and tries to look into the future from the point of view of 23 August 1939, it is difficult to see what other course Soviet Russia could have followed. The Soviet apprehensions of a European alliance against Russia were exaggerated, though not groundless. But, quite apart from this — given the Polish refusal of Soviet aid, given too the British policy of drawing out negotiations in Moscow without seriously striving for a conclusion — neutrality, with or without a formal pact, was the most that Soviet diplomacy could attain; and limitation of German gains in Poland and the Baltic was the inducement which made a formal pact attractive. . . .

At any rate the bomb had exploded. Hitler was radiant, confident that he had pulled off the decisive stroke. On 22 August he entertained his leading generals to the wildest of his speeches. "Close your hearts to pity. Act brutally." This rigmarole was not a serious directive for action — no formal record was kept. Hitler was glorying in his own skill. Tucked away in the speech was a hard core. "Now the probability is great that the West will not intervene." As well, Hitler was talking for effect. A report of the speech reached the British embassy almost at once; whether intentionally or not, the so-called German "resistance" did Hitler's work for him. On 23 August Hitler took a further step. He fixed the attack on Poland for 4.40 a.m. on 26 August. This, too, was play-acting to impress the generals and, through them, the Western Powers. The German timetable could operate only from 1 September. Before then an attack on Poland was possible only if she had already surrendered.

But technical considerations no longer seemed to matter: the Nazi-Soviet pact was assumed to have cleared the way for a diplomatic collapse on the part of the Western Powers. . . .

In England, however, events did not come up to Hitler's expectation. Quite the reverse. Parliament met on 24 August, and unanimously applauded what it supposed to be the government's firm stand. Hitler began to have doubts: evidently more was needed to extract from the British government the concessions on which he still counted. On 24 August Hitler flew to Berlin. On his instructions, Goering called in the Swede Dahlerus, and sent him off to London with an unofficial appeal for British mediation. This was an ingenious trap: if the British refused, Hitler could claim that he had never made a move; if they yielded, they would be compelled to put pressure on Poland. The same evening Hitler held a meeting with Goering, Ribbentrop, and the principal generals. Should they go on with the attack on Poland, now due to begin within thirty-six hours? Hitler declared that he would make a further attempt to detach the Western Powers from their Polish allies. The attempt took the form of a "last offer," communicated to Henderson shortly after noon on 25 August. Germany, Hitler declared, was determined "to abolish the Macedonian conditions on her eastern frontier." The problems of Danzig and the Corridor must be solved — though he still did not say how. Once these problems were out of the way, Germany would make "a large, comprehensive offer"; she would guarantee the British Empire, accept an agreed limitation of armaments, and renew the assurance that her frontier in the west was final. Henderson was impressed, as usual. Hitler, he reported, spoke "with great earnestness and apparent sincerity." Later writers have all dismissed Hitler's offer as fraudulent; and so in a sense it was. The immediate object was to isolate Poland. Yet the offer also represented Hitler's permanent policy: though he wanted a free hand to destroy conditions in the east which enlightened Western opinion had also pronounced intolerable, he had no ambitions directed against Great Britain and France. . . .

Thus the two sides circled round each other like wrestlers seeking advantage before the clinch. The British offered to arrange direct negotiations between Germany and Poland if Hitler would promise to behave peacefully; Hitler replied that there would be no war if he got his way over Danzig. Later writers have argued that Hitler's reply was dishonest; that he was concerned to isolate Poland, not to avoid war. This may well be true. But the offer by the British government was dishonest also: there was no chance of extracting concessions from the Poles once the danger of war was removed, and the British knew it. . .

The deadlock lasted until 29 August. Then it was broken by Hitler. He was in the weaker position, though the British did not know it. There was not much time left before 1 September for him to pull off diplomatic success. At 7.15 p.m. he made to Henderson a formal offer and a formal demand: he would negotiate directly with Poland if a Polish plenipotentiary arrived in Berlin the following day. This was a retreat from the position Hitler had rigorously asserted since 26 March — that he would never again deal directly with the Poles. Though Henderson complained that the demand was perilously near an ultimatum, he was eager to accept it; it constituted in his opinion the "sole chance of preventing war." Henderson pressed the demand on his own government; he urged the French government to advise an immediate visit by Beck; he was most insistent of all with the Polish ambassador Lipski. Lipski took no notice — apparently he did not even report Hitler's demand to Warsaw. The French government responded as clearly in the opposite direction — they told Beck to go to Berlin at once. But the decision rested with the British government. Here was the proposal which they had always

wanted and which they had repeatedly hinted at to Hitler: direct negotiations between Poland and Germany. Hitler had now done his part; but they could not do theirs. They had the gravest doubt whether the Poles would thus present themselves in Berlin at Hitler's behest. Kennedy reported Chamberlain's feeling to Washington: "Frankly he is more worried about getting the Poles to be reasonable than the Germans." The British gnawed over the problem throughout 30 August. Finally they hit on a sort of solution. They passed Hitler's demand on to Warsaw at 12.25 a.m. on 31 August — that is to say, twenty-five minutes after the German ultimatum, if such it were, had expired. The British had been correct in their apprehension of Polish obstinacy. Beck, when informed of Hitler's demand, at once replied: "if invited to Berlin he would of course not go, as he had no intention of being treated like President Hácha." Thus the British, by acting too late, could still claim that they had offered something which they knew they could not deliver: a Polish plenipotentiary in Berlin.

Hitler had not anticipated this. He had expected that negotiations would start; and he then intended them to break down on Polish obstinacy. On his instructions detailed demands were at last prepared. These were principally the immediate return of Danzig, and a plebiscite in the Corridor — the very terms which the British and French governments had themselves long favoured. But, failing a Polish plenipotentiary, the Germans had difficulty in making their terms known. At midnight on 30 August Henderson brought to Ribbentrop the news that a Polish plenipotentiary was not coming that day. Ribbentrop had only the rough draft of the proposed German terms, scribbled over with Hitler's emendations. It was not in a condition to be shown to Henderson; and Ribbentrop had instructions from Hitler not to do so. He therefore read the terms over slowly. Later a myth grew up that he had "gabbled" them, deliberately cheating Henderson with terms that were only for show. In fact Henderson got the gist clearly, and was impressed. Taken at their face value, he thought, they were "not unreasonable." On his return to the British embassy, he summoned Lipski at 2 a.m., and urged him to seek an interview with Ribbentrop at once. Lipski took no notice, and went back to bed.

The Germans were now anxious that their terms had not gone properly on record with Henderson. They once more employed Dahlerus as an allegedly unofficial emissary. Goering, claiming to be acting in defiance of Hitler, showed the terms to Dahlerus, who in turn telephoned them to the British embassy about 4 a.m. Since Goering knew that all telephone conversations were monitored by at least three government agencies (one of them his own), his defiance of Hitler was of course a fiction. The next morning Goering abandoned it. Dahlerus was given a copy of the German terms, and took it round to the British embassy. Henderson again summoned Lipski, who refused to come. Dahlerus and Ogilvie-Forbes, the British counsellor of embassy, were dispatched to see Lipski. He remained unmoved. He refused to look at the German terms. When Dahlerus was out of the room, Lipski protested against introducing this intermediary, and said: "he would stake his reputation that German morale was breaking and that the present régime would soon crack. . . . This German offer was a trap. It was also a sign of weakness on the part of the Germans." In a further effort to break through the crust of obstinacy, Dahlerus telephoned to Horace Wilson in London. The German terms, he said, were "extremely liberal"; it was "'obvious to us' [Dahlerus? Goering? Henderson?] that the Poles were obstructing the possibilities of a negotiation." Wilson realised that the Germans were listening-in; he told Dahlerus to shut up and put down the receiver.

The precaution came too late. Every move of the last few hours had been as public as if it had been announced in the newspapers. The telephone calls between Henderson and Lipski, and between Dahlerus and Henderson, the comings and goings between the British and Polish embassies — all these were known to the Germans. They were undoubtedly known to Hitler. What conclusion could he possibly draw? Only the conclusion that he had succeeded in driving a wedge between Poland and her Western allies. This was true in regard to the French government. It was true in regard to Henderson. He wrote late on 31 August: "On German offer war would be completely unjustifiable. . . . Polish Government should announce tomorrow, in the light of German proposals which have now been made public, their intention to send a Plenipotentiary to discuss in general terms these proposals." Hitler was not to know that Henderson no longer carried the weight in London which he had carried the year before. But even the British government were losing patience with the Poles. Late on the night of 31 August Halifax telegraphed to Warsaw: "I do not see why the Polish Government should feel difficulty about authorising Polish Ambassador to accept a document from the German Government." Given another twenty-four hours, and the breach would be wide open. But Hitler had not got the twenty-four hours. He was the prisoner of his own time-table. With his generals watching sceptically, he could not again call off the attack of Poland unless he had something solid to show; and this was still denied him by the Poles. The breach between Poland and her allies gave him a chance. He had to gamble on it.

At 12.40 p.m. on 31 August Hitler decided that the attack should proceed. At 1 p.m. Lipski telephoned, asking for an interview with Ribbentrop. The Germans, who had intercepted his instructions, knew that he had been told not to enter into "any concrete negotiations." At 3 p.m. Weizsäcker telephoned Lipski to ask whether he was coming as a plenipotentiary. Lipski replied: "No, in his capacity as an ambassador." This was enough for Hitler. The Poles, it seemed, were remaining obstinate;

he could go forward to the gamble of isolating them in war. At 4 p.m. the orders for war were confirmed. At 6.30 p.m. Lipski at last saw Ribbentrop. Lipski said that his government were "favourably considering" the British proposal for direct Polish-German negotiations. Ribbentrop asked whether he was a plenipotentiary. Lipski again answered No. Ribbentrop did not communicate the German terms; if he had tried to do so, Lipski would have refused to receive them. Thus ended the only direct contact between Germany and Poland since 26 March. The Poles had kept their nerve unbroken to the last moment. At 4.45 a.m. on the following morning the German attack on Poland began. At 6 a.m. German aeroplanes bombed Warsaw.

Here was a clear *casus foederis* for both Great Britain and France. Their ally had been wantonly attacked; it only remained for them to declare war on the aggressor. Nothing of the kind happened. Both governments addressed a pained remonstrance to Hitler, warning him that they would have to go to war unless he desisted. Meanwhile they waited for something to turn up; and something did. On 31 August Mussolini, carefully following the precedent of the previous year, proposed a European conference: it should meet on 5 September and should survey all causes of European conflict, with the precondition that Danzig should return to Germany in advance. The two Western governments were favourable to the proposal when it first reached them. But Mussolini had got his timing wrong. In 1938 he had three days in which to avert war; in 1939 less than twenty-four hours, and this was not enough. By 1 September, when the Western governments replied to Mussolini, they had to postulate that fighting must first stop in Poland. Nor was this all. While Bonnet was enthusiastic for Mussolini's proposal, in Great Britain public opinion took charge. The House of Commons was restive when Chamberlain explained that Germany had merely been "warned"; it expected something more solid next day. Halifax, swing-

ing as usual with the national mood, insisted that the conference could be held only if Germany withdrew from all Polish territory. The Italians knew that it was hopeless to place such a demand before Hitler; they dropped the conference without further effort.

Yet both the British and French governments, the French especially, went on believing in a conference which had vanished before it was born. Hitler had initially replied to Mussolini that, if invited to a conference, he would give his answer at midday on 3 September. Therefore Bonnet, and Chamberlain with him, strove desperately to postpone a declaration of war until after that time, even though the Italians no longer intended to invite Hitler or anyone else. Bonnet conjured up the excuse that the French military wanted the delay in order to carry through mobilisation, undisturbed by German air attack (which, they knew, would not occur anyway — the German air force was fully employed in Poland). Chamberlain conjured up no excuse except that the French wanted delay and that it was always difficult to work with allies. In the evening of 2 September he was still entertaining the House of Commons with hypothetical negotiations: "If the German Government should agree to withdraw their forces then His Majesty's Government would be willing to regard the position as being the same as it was before the German forces crossed the Polish frontier. That is to say, the way would be open to discussion between the German and Polish Governments on the matters at issue." This was too much even for loyal Conservatives. Leo Amery called to Arthur Greenwood, acting leader of the Opposition: "Speak for England," a task of which Chamberlain was incapable. Ministers, led by Halifax, warned Chamberlain that the government would fall unless it sent an ultimatum to Hitler before the House met again. Chamberlain gave way. The objections of the French were overruled. The British ultimatum was delivered to the Germans at 9 a.m. on 3 September. It expired at 11 a.m., and a state of war followed. When Bonnet learnt that the British were going to war in any case, his overriding anxiety was to catch up with them. The time of the French ultimatum was advanced, despite the supposed objections of the General Staff: it was delivered at noon on 3 September and expired at 5 p.m. In this curious way the French who had preached resistance to Germany for twenty years appeared to be dragged into war by the British who had for twenty years preached conciliation. Both countries went to war for that part of the peace settlement which they had long regarded as least defensible. Hitler may have projected a great war all along; yet it seems from the record that he became involved in war through launching on 29 August a diplomatic manoeuvre which he ought to have launched on 28 August.

Such were the origins of the second World war, or rather of the war between the three Western Powers over the settlement of Versailles; a war which had been implicit since the moment when the first war ended. Men will long debate whether this renewed war could have been averted by greater firmness or by greater conciliation; and no answer will be found to these hypothetical speculations. Maybe either would have succeeded, if consistently followed; the mixture of the two, practised by the British government, was the most likely to fail. . . .

HITLER'S PLAN FOR WAR REAFFIRMED

HUGH R. TREVOR-ROPER

It is possible that A. J. P. Taylor's chief motive in publishing *The Origins of the Second World War* was to reawaken historical debate about the coming of war in 1939. This and other possible motives are suggested by Hugh R. Trevor-Roper in this reading, which reproduces in full a substantial review of the Taylor book. Whatever the historian's motive, limits imposed by scholarly methodology—including respect for critically established evidence—must not be disregarded by a responsible scholar. Taylor has clearly disregarded scholarly canons, argues the author of this review. In a sense Trevor-Roper is defending his own position against implied attack by the Taylor volume. For in his colorful account of *The Last Days of Hitler* (1947) and other writings, Trevor-Roper has interpreted Hitler as a man possessed by a demonic spirit or psychic disorder, whose guilt for the outbreak of the Second World War was unique and beyond question. Trevor-Roper is Regius Professor of Modern History at Oxford University. How convincing is his criticism of the Taylor volume? How convincing is the Taylor volume in the light of Trevor-Roper's criticism?

I T is over twenty years since the war began. A generation has grown up which never knew the 1930's, never shared its passions and doubts, was never excited by the Spanish civil war, never boiled with indignation against the "appeasers," never lived in suspense from Nuremberg Rally to Nuremberg Rally, awaiting the next hysterical outburst, the next clatter of arms, from the megalomaniac in Berlin. Those of us who knew those days and who try to teach this new generation are constantly made aware of this great gulf between us. How can we communicate across such a gulf the emotional content of those years, the mounting indignation which finally convinced even the "appeasers" themselves that there could be no peace with Hitler, and caused the British people, united in pacifism in 1936, to go, in 1939, united into war? For it was not the differing shades of justice in Germany's claims upon the Rhineland, Austria, the Sudetenland, Prague, and Danzig which caused men who had swallowed the first of these annexations to be increasingly exasperated by those which followed and take up arms against the last. It was a changing mood, a growing conviction that all such claims were but pretexts under which Hitler pursued not justice or self-determination for Germany but world-conquest, and that, now or never, he must be stopped. And even across the gulf such a mood must be conveyed by those who teach history to those who learn it: for it is an element in history no less important than the mere facts.

Or is it? Mr. A. J. P. Taylor, it seems, does not think so. He sees the gulf all right, and he wishes to speak to those on the other side of it; but in order to do so, he has decided to lighten the weight he must carry with him. Stripping himself of

H. R. Trevor-Roper, "A. J. P. Taylor, Hitler, and the War," *Encounter*, XVII (July, 1961), 88–96. Reprinted by permission of Professor Trevor-Roper, his literary agent (A. D. Peters), and the editors of *Encounter*.

all personal memories, and thus making himself, in this respect, as naked as they are, he has jumped nimbly across the gulf and now presents himself to them as the first enlightened historian of the future, capable of interpreting the politics of the 1920's and 1930's without any reference to the emotions they engendered, even in himself. Their sole guide, he tells them, must be the documents, which he will select and interpret for them; and indeed, by selection and interpretation, he presents them with a new thesis, illustrated (we need hardly say) with all his old resources of learning, paradox, and *gaminerie*.

The thesis is perfectly clear. According to Mr. Taylor, Hitler was an ordinary German statesman in the tradition of Stresemann and Brüning, differing from them not in methods (he was made Chancellor for "solidly democratic reasons") nor in ideas (he had no ideas) but only in the greater patience and stronger nerves with which he took advantage of the objective situation in Europe. His policy, in so far as he had a policy, was no different from that of his predecessors. He sought neither war nor annexation of territory. He merely sought to restore Germany's "natural" position in Europe, which had been artificially altered by the Treaty of Versailles: a treaty which, for that reason, "lacked moral validity from the start." Such a restoration might involve the recovery of lost German territory like Danzig, but it did not entail the direct government even of Austria or the Sudetenland, let alone Bohemia. Ideally, all that Hitler required was that Austria, Czechoslovakia, and other small Central European states, while remaining independent, should become political satellites of Germany.

Of course it did not work out thus. But that, we are assured, was not Hitler's fault. For Hitler, according to Mr. Taylor, never took the initiative in politics. He "did not make plans — for world-conquest or anything else. He assumed that others would provide opportunities and that he would seize them." And that is what happened.

The Austrian crisis of March 1938, we are told, "was provoked by Schuschnigg, not by Hitler." Hitler was positively embarrassed by it: "he was Austrian enough to find the complete disappearance of Austria inconceivable until it happened." Similarly we learn that the Sudeten crisis of 1938 was created by the Sudeten Nazis, who "built up the tension gradually, without guidance from Hitler": Hitler himself "merely took advantage of it." Having taken advantage of it at Munich, he had no intention of going on and annexing the Czech lands: "he merely doubted whether the settlement would work . . . [he] believed, without sinister intention, that independent Czechoslovakia could not survive when deprived of her natural frontiers and with Czech prestige broken." So, within six months, as "the unforeseen by-product of developments in Slovakia," he felt obliged to tear up the settlement and occupy Prague; but there was "nothing sinister or premeditated" in that. It was an unfortunate necessity forced upon him by the unskilful President Hácha. The Polish crisis of 1939 was similarly forced upon him by Beck. "The destruction of Poland," we are told, "had been no part of his original project. On the contrary, he wished to solve the question of Danzig so that Germany and Poland could remain on good terms." The last thing he wanted was war. The war of nerves was "the only war he understood and liked." Germany "was not equipped to conquer Europe."

The state of German rearmament in 1939 gives the decisive proof that Hitler was not contemplating general war, and probably not contemplating war at all.

Even on August 23rd, 1939, when the Nazi-Soviet Pact was signed, "both Hitler and Stalin imagined that they had prevented war, not brought it on." What rational person could have supposed that this pact, instead of discouraging the British, would determine them to stand by their commitments? The war, "far from being premeditated, was a mistake, the result on both sides of diplomatic blunders."

Hitler's own share of these diplomatic blunders was, it seems, very small. He "became involved in war," we are told, "through launching on August 29th a diplomatic manœuvre which he ought to have launched on August 28th." The blunders of the Western statesmen were far more fundamental. For what ought the Western statesmen to have done when faced by Hitler's modest demands? According to Mr. Taylor, they should have conceded them all. They should not have conceded anything to Mussolini, for Mussolini's demands were essentially different from Hitler's. Mussolini was "a vain, blustering boaster" whose government, unlike the "solidly democratic" rule of Hitler, "lived in a state of illegality," and whose demands, since they did not correspond with "reality," were "a fraud." Western statesmen, says Mr. Taylor, lost all claim to respect by recognising such a man. But Hitler was a statesman who merely sought to reassert Germany's "natural weight," and they would therefore have gained respect by recognising him. Accordingly Mr. Taylor's heroes among Western statesmen are those who recognised German claims: Ramsay MacDonald and Neville Chamberlain. Winston Churchill believed in the balance of power and would have maintained frontiers designed on principles of security, not nationality. Intolerable cynicism! How much nobler was that "triumph for British policy," the Munich settlement!

It was a triumph for all that was best and most enlightened in British life; a triumph for those who had preached equal justice between peoples; a triumph for those who had courageously denounced the harshness and shortsightedness of Versailles.

Munich, according to Mr. Taylor, "atoned" for all the previous weakness of British policy; it was a victory for "morality" (which is his word for political realism); and he praises Chamberlain's "skill

and persistence" in bringing "first the French and then the Czechs to follow the moral line." If only Chamberlain had not lost his nerve in 1939! If only he had shown equal "skill and persistence" in enabling Hitler to detach Danzig and the Polish Corridor, how happy we should all be! Germany would have recovered its "natural" position, "morality" would have triumphed, and everyone would be happy in the best of possible worlds.

Such, in brief, is Mr. Taylor's thesis. It is not surprising that it has been hailed with cries of delight in neo-Nazi or semi-Nazi circles in Germany. It is more surprising that the book has been greeted by the fashionable Grub Street of England as the highest achievement of British historiography. Mr. Taylor has been compared with Gibbon and Macaulay; his failure to secure worthy promotion has caused astonishment. The anonymous oracle of the *Times Literary Supplement* has predicted finality for the result of his "methodical and impeccable logic." In the *Observer*, Mr. Sebastian Haffner (who recently published a panegyric of that "greatest Roman of them all," Dr. Goebbels) has declared the book "an almost faultless masterpiece" in which "fairness reigns supreme"; and his cosy, middlebrow colleagues in rival papers, hypnotised by a reputation which they are unqualified to test, have obediently jollied their readers along in harmony with the blurb. However, let us not all be hypnotised. Before hurling ourselves down the Gadarene slope, let us ask of Mr. Taylor's thesis, not, Is it brilliant? Is it plausible? but, Is it true? By what rules of evidence, by what philosophy of interpretation is it reached?

Perhaps we may begin by noting Mr. Taylor's general philosophy. Mr. Taylor, it seems, does not believe that human agents matter much in history. His story is "a story without heroes, and perhaps even without villains." "In my opinion," he explains, "statesmen are too absorbed by events to follow a preconceived plan. They take one step and the next follows from it." If they achieve anything, it is by accident, not design: "all statesmen aim to win: the size of their winnings often surprises them." The real determinants of history, according to Mr. Taylor, are objective situations and human blunders. Objective situations consist of the realities of power; human intelligence is best employed in recognising these realities and allowing events to conform with them; but as human intelligence seldom prevails in politics, the realities generally have to assert themselves, at greater human cost, through the mess caused by human blunders. This doctrine (if I have correctly expressed it) seems remarkably like Mr. E. H. Carr's "realist" doctrine, advanced in his book *The Twenty Years' Crisis* (1938) — see the *first* edition — a book rightly described by Mr. Taylor as "a brilliant argument in favour of appeasement."

Once we accept this general theory, the next stage is easy. All we have to do is to ask ourselves, at what point do we make our calculation of reality? This then provides us with a *datum*. Mr. Taylor takes as his *datum* the spring of 1918. At that time Germany was victorious in the West and triumphant in the East. This, he implies, was the "natural" situation: the Allied victory later in 1918 was artificial — or at least it was made artificial (or, in his words, deprived of "moral validity") by the failure of the Allies to carve Germany up before making peace. This omission left Germany still potentially the greatest power in Europe, naturally tending to revert to the "real" position of January 1918. All that intelligent German statesmen had to do, or indeed could do, was to work hand-in-glove with this "historical necessity" — to their profit. All that Allied statesmen could do was to yield to the same necessity — to their loss. In this sense Hitler and Chamberlain were intelligent statesmen.

But is this general philosophy true? Do statesmen really never make history? Are they, all of them, always "too absorbed by events to follow a preconceived plan"? Was

this true of Richelieu, of Bismarck, of Lenin? In particular, was it true of Hitler? Was Hitler really just a more violent Mr. Micawber sitting in Berlin or Berchtesgaden and waiting for something to turn up: something which, thanks to historic necessity, he could then turn to advantage? Certainly Hitler himself did not think so. He regarded himself as a thinker, a practical philosopher, the demiurge of a new age of history. And since he published a blueprint of the policy which he intended to carry out, ought we not at least to look at this blueprint just in case it had some relevance to his policy? After all, the reason why the majority of the British people reluctantly changed, between 1936 and 1939, from the views of Neville Chamberlain and Mr. Taylor to the views of Winston Churchill was their growing conviction that Hitler meant what he said: that he was aiming — *so oder so*, as he used to say — at world conquest. A contemporary conviction that was strong enough to change the mood of a nation from a passionate desire for peace to a resolute determination on war surely deserves some respect from the historian. A historian who totally ignores it because, twenty years later, he can interpret some of the documents in an opposite sense runs the risk of being considered too clever by half.

Let us consider briefly the programme which Hitler laid down for himself. It was a programme of Eastern colonisation, entailing a war of conquest against Russia. If it were successfully carried out, it would leave Germany dominant in Eurasia and able to conquer the West at will. In order to carry it out, Hitler needed a restored German army which, since it must be powerful enough to conquer Russia, must also be powerful enough to conquer the West if that should be necessary. And that might be necessary even before the attack on Russia. For in order to reach Russia, Hitler would need to send his armies through Poland; and in order to do this — whether by the conquest of Poland or in alliance with it — he would need to break the bonds of treaty and interest which bound the new countries of Eastern Europe, the creatures of Versailles, to their creators, Britain and France. Hitler might be able to break those bonds without war against the West, but he could not be sure of it: it was always possible that a war with the West would be necessary before he could march against Russia. And in fact this is what happened.

Now this programme, which Hitler ascribed to himself, and which he actually carried out, is obviously entirely different from the far more limited programme which is ascribed to him by Mr. Taylor, and which he did not carry out. How then does Mr. Taylor deal with the evidence about it? He deals with it quite simply, either by ignoring it or by denying it as inconsistent with his own theories about statesmen in general and Hitler in particular: theories (one must add) for which he produces no evidence at all.

Take the inconvenient fact of Hitler's avowed programme of a great Eastern land-empire. In spite of some casual admission, Mr. Taylor effectively denies that Hitler had any such programme. Hitler, he says, "was always the man of daring improvisations: he made lightning decisions and then presented them as the result of long-term policy." Hitler's *Table Talk,* he says airily (as if this were the only evidence for such a programme), "was delivered far in occupied territory during the campaign against Soviet Russia, and *then* Hitler dreamed of some fantastic empire which would rationalise his career of conquest." [My italics here, and in all quotations below.] But why does Mr. Taylor believe, or rather pretend, that it was only in 1942, after his Russian conquests, that Hitler dreamed of an Eastern Empire? His programme had been stated, as clearly as possible, in 1924, in *Mein Kampf,* and on numerous other occasions since. Mr. Taylor hardly ever refers to *Mein Kampf* and never to the other occasions. In 1939, he admits, some people "attributed" to Hitler "grandi-

ose plans which *they claimed* to have discovered by reading *Mein Kampf* in the original (Hitler forbade its publication in English)." The implication is that such plans are not to be found in *Mein Kampf* and that those who "claimed to have discovered" them had not really read, or been able to read, an untranslated work. But the fact is that those plans are unmistakably stated in *Mein Kampf* and that all the evidence of the 1930's showed that Hitler still intended to carry them out. I may add (since Mr. Taylor includes me among those who have ascribed to Hitler "preconceived plans" which he never pursued) that I myself read *Mein Kampf* in the original in 1938, and that I read it under the impact of Munich and of the remarkable prophecies of Sir Robert Ensor, who had read it and who insisted that Hitler meant what he said. By absolutely refusing to face this evidence, and contemptuously dismissing those who have faced it, Mr. Taylor contrives to reach the preposterous conclusion that men like Ensor, who correctly forecast Hitler's future programme from the evidence, were really wrong, and that men like Chamberlain, who did not read the evidence and were proved totally wrong by events, were really right. His sole justification of this paradox is that he has accepted as an axiom a characterisation of Hitler as a "traditional" statesman pursuing limited aims. Mr. Taylor's Hitler cannot have held such views, and therefore the inconvenient fact that the real Hitler uttered such views with remarkable consistency for twenty years and actually put them into practice, is simply puffed aside. When Hitler, in 1941, finally launched that conquest of Russia which, as he himself said, was "the be-all and end-all of Nazism," Mr. Taylor easily explains it away. "By 1941," he says, "Hitler had lost his old gift of patience": he "gratuitously" deviated from his former course; and at the mere thought of such an unaccountable fall from grace, Mr. Taylor promptly ends his book.

Nor is this the only perversion of evidence to which Mr. Taylor has to resort, in order to represent Hitler as a "traditional" statesman. The traditional statesmen *did not seek*, as Hitler did, to incorporate the Sudeten Germans in the Reich. Traditional statesmen demanded the frontiers of 1914; but Hitler, again and again, repudiated the frontiers of 1914 as a contemptible ambition. They looked back, at most, to the war-aims of 1914; he repudiated those war-aims. Even the "natural" position of January 1918, after the huge gains of Brest-Litovsk, was insufficient for Hitler. The treaty of Brest-Litovsk gave Germany the Ukraine as a colony of exploitation, a capitalist colony. But Hitler always made it quite clear that he spurned such a colony: he wanted the Ukraine as a colony of settlement. "I should deem it a crime," he said, "if I sacrificed the blood of a quarter of a million men merely for the conquest of natural riches to be exploited in a capitalist way. The goal of the *Ostpolitik* is to open up an area of settlement for a hundred million Germans." All this is pushed aside by Mr. Taylor with the remark,

when Hitler lamented, "If only we had a Ukraine . . ." he seemed to suppose there were no Ukrainians. Did he propose to exploit, or exterminate them? *Apparently he never considered the question.*

As if Hitler had not made his answer perfectly plain! As if he had any scruples about transporting or even exterminating populations! What about the European Jews? But that episode is conveniently forgottten by Mr. Taylor. It does not fit the character of a traditional German statesman who "in principle and doctrine, was no more wicked and unscrupulous than many other contemporary statesmen."

If Mr. Taylor's cardinal assumptions about Hitler's character and purpose are, to say the least, questionable, what are we to say of his use of evidence to illustrate them? Here he states his method with admirable clarity. "It is an elementary part of historical discipline," he says, "to ask of a docu-

ment not only what is in it but why it came into existence." With this maxim we may agree, only adding that since the contents of a document are objective evidence while its purpose may be a matter of private surmise, we must not rashly subject the former to the latter. Sometimes a man may say the truth even in a document called forth by tactical necessity. At all events, we are not entitled, in defence of an already paradoxical general theory, to assume that he is lying simply because it may not be tactically necessary for him, at that moment, to utter nothing but the truth.

Now let us take a few instances. On November 5th, 1937, Hitler summoned his war-leaders to the Chancellery and made a speech which, he said, in the event of his death was to be regarded as his "last will and testament." That suggests that he was not talking irresponsibly. The official record of this speech is the so-called "Hossbach Memorandum" which was used at Nuremberg as evidence of Hitler's plans for the gradual conquest of Europe. In it Hitler declared that the aim of German policy must be the conquest of *Lebensraum* in Europe, "but we will not copy liberal capitalist policies which rely on exploiting colonies. It is not a case of conquering people but of conquering agriculturally useful space." That seems clear enough. Then Hitler went on to consider the means of making such conquests. "German politics," he said "must reckon with two hateful enemies, England and France, to whom a strong German colossus in the centre of Europe would be intolerable." Moreover, he admitted, these two hateful enemies would probably, at some stage, resist him by force: "the German question can only be solved by way of force, and this is never without risk." He then proceeded to discuss hypothetical possibilities. Since the hypothetical circumstances did not in fact arise, we need not dwell on them. The essential points are that the risk of European war must be faced by 1943–5, for "after that we can only expect a change fo the worse," and that "our *first* aim" mu be, at the first convenient opportunity, "to conquer Czechoslovakia and Austria simultaneously." This first conquest he hoped to achieve without war, for "in all probability England and perhaps also France have already silently written off Czechoslovakia." It could and should therefore be attempted as soon as circumstances make it possible in order that the later, more real risk could be faced before 1943–5. But there was to be no doubt about the nature of the conquest. It was not to be (as Mr. Taylor always maintains) the reduction of Austria and Czechoslovakia to the role of satellites: it was to be, in Hitler's own words, "the annexation of the two states to Germany, militarily and politically." The idea of satellite states in Eastern Europe, Hitler said in a secret speech delivered only a fortnight later, was one of the futile notions of "traditional" German politicians, and he dismissed it as "idiotic" (wahnsinnig). Finally, it is clear that conquered Austria and Czechoslovakia cannot themselves have constituted the Lebensraum which was the ultimate objective. Austria and Czechoslovakia were to be stepping-stones, "in all probability" secured without war, towards larger conquests which would entail a greater risk.

Such was Hitler's "testament" of November 1937. Its content is clear and logical and it has been taken seriously by all historians — until Mr. Taylor comes along and tells us that we have all been hoodwinked. For was not this document produced at Nuremberg? All documents produced at Nuremberg, he says, are "loaded," and "anyone who relies on them finds it almost impossible to escape from the load with which they are charged." So Mr. Taylor gives us a sample of his method of using such documents. Why, he asks, was the speech made? "The historian," he observes, "must push through the cloud of phrases" (so much for Hitler's perfectly clear statements) "to the realities beneath." The speech, he notes, was not made to but to generals and admirals, and its was clearly to demand greater re-

armament. With this we can agree. But Mr. Taylor does not stop there. In order to persuade these "conservative" war-leaders of the necessity of further rearmament, Hitler (he says) had to overcome the economic opposition of Dr. Schacht. His speech therefore "had no other purpose" than "to isolate Schacht from the other conservatives"; the dates 1943–5 (to which Hitler consistently kept) "like all such figures, really meant 'this year, next year, sometime . . .'"; and the content of a speech which Hitler himself described as his political testament (but Mr. Taylor does not quote that description) is dismissed as "daydreaming unrelated to what followed in real life." Why Hitler should be expected to speak more "realistically" on military matters to Nazis at a froth-blowers' meeting than to hard-headed war-leaders who would have to organise and carry out his programme is not clear. Presumably it is "an elementary part of historical discipline" to assume that.

A second example of Mr. Taylor's "historical discipline" is provided by his treatment of the crisis leading to the outbreak of war in 1939. By now Austria and Czechoslovakia had been "annexed to Germany, militarily and politically," and Hitler had turned the heat upon Poland. According to Mr. Taylor, Hitler really only wanted the German city of Danzig, but since geography prevented him from obtaining it except by the coercion of Poland, he was forced, reluctantly, to apply such coercion and prepare military plans. Of course (according to Mr. Taylor) he did not intend to execute these plans. His military plans were "only intended to reinforce the diplomatic war of nerves." Unfortunately the British Government, misled after Hitler's occupation of Prague into thinking that he aimed at far larger conquests, had imprudently guaranteed Poland and thus threatened Hitler with European war if he sought this next "natural," "moral" aim by any but peaceful means. However, Hitler was a match for this. By making his pact with Russia, he effectively countered the British guarantee, and therefore, pushing, like Mr. Taylor, "through the cloud of phrases to the realities beneath," he ignored its empty words and relied, as a rational man, on "the crumbling of Western nerve." Unfortunately, in this case, he miscalculated. Britain, quixotically faithful to the "phrases" of the guarantee, and deluded by the idea that Hitler, if given a free hand, would not stop at Danzig, ignored all the "realities" of the situation and made war, "war for Danzig."

Such is Mr. Taylor's version of the Polish crisis. In defence of it he finds it necessary here, too, to charm away some important documents, and once again it is instructive to watch the exorcist at work. On May 23rd, 1939, Hitler again summoned his war-leaders. He told them, according to Mr. Taylor, who quotes no other words of the document, "there will be war. Our task is to isolate Poland. . . . It must not come to a simultaneous showdown with the West." "This," comments Mr. Taylor, "seems clear enough"; but he then dismisses even this evidence by saying authoritatively that "when Hitler talked to his generals, he talked for effect, not to reveal the workings of his mind." So that is that. Three months later, with the signature of the Nazi-Soviet Pact, Hitler again addressed his generals, and again Mr. Taylor is content to quote only one sentence from the speech: "now the probability is great that the West will not intervene." Apart from that "hard core," the rest of the speech, he says, can be ignored, as Hitler "was talking for effect." After all, by the Nazi-Soviet Pact, Hitler considered that "he had prevented war, not brought it on." So, once again, Hitler's mere "phrases" dissolve on contact with Mr. Taylor's "realities."

But why should we suppose, as an axiom, that Hitler, when briefing his generals on the eve of a possible war, talked only for effect? Why should we not suppose that he intended them to be ready (as they were) for the real future? And why should we altogether overlook some very clear statements which he made to them? For if we look at the full texts of these two

speeches, we find that Mr. Taylor has made certain remarkable omissions.

In the first of these two speeches Hitler began by insisting that the next step towards Germany's goal could not be taken "without the invasion of foreign states or attacks upon foreign property," and that although bloodless victories had been won in the past, "further successes cannot be obtained without the shedding of blood." "*Danzig,*" he went on, in words from which Mr. Taylor has firmly averted his eyes, "*is not the subject of the dispute at all*. It is a question of expanding our living-space in the East." Moreover, he looked clearly forward to the prospect of war with the West. "The Polish problem," he said, "is inseparable from conflict with the West." For all that, "we are left with the decision to attack Poland at the first opportunity. We cannot expect a repetition of the Czech affair." Of course Hitler hoped to avoid a simultaneous conflict with the West, but he did not rely on any such hope: "the *Führer* doubts the possibility of a peaceful settlement with England. We must prepare ourselves for the conflict." The remaining two-thirds of the document deal with the problems of war with Britain, "the driving-force against Germany." All this is totally ignored by Mr. Taylor: it cannot have been the "hard core" of any argument used by *his* Hitler: therefore, he declares, it was mere froth, uttered for "effect."

In the second speech Hitler similarly made clear statements which Mr. Taylor does not quote. For instance, immediately after the "hard core," the single sentence which he does quote, about the probability that the West will be frightened out of intervention by the Nazi-Soviet Pact, come the words, "*we must accept the risk with reckless resolution*"; and Hitler then went on to explain how Germany, thanks to Russian supplies, could withstand a Western blockade. His only fear, he said, was that "at the last moment some *Schweinhund* will make a proposal for mediation": a proposal, perhaps, which might have fobbed him off with Danzig which, as he had admitted, was "not the subject of the dispute at all." No: Hitler was now resolved on war, even if the West did come in.

I shall give a propagandist cause for starting the war: never mind if it be plausible or not. The victor shall not be asked afterwards whether he told the truth or not.

As for the West, "even if war should break out in the West, the destruction of Poland shall be the primary objective." Which indeed was exactly what happened. By last-minute diplomatic manœuvres Hitler naturally sought to detach the West, but when that could not be done, he went ahead, with his eyes open, into a European war which, though larger than he had hoped, he still reckoned on winning.

I have said enough to show why I think Mr. Taylor's book utterly erroneous. In spite of his statements about "historical discipline," he selects, suppresses, and arranges evidence on no principle other than the needs of his thesis; and that thesis, that Hitler was a traditional statesman, of limited aims, merely responding to a given situation, rests on no evidence at all, ignores essential evidence, and is, in my opinion, demonstrably false. This casuistical defence of Hitler's foreign policy will not only do harm by supporting neo-Nazi mythology: it will also do harm, perhaps irreparable harm, to Mr. Taylor's reputation as a serious historian.

But why, we may ask, has he written it? Is it, as some have suggested, a gesture of posthumous defiance to his former master, Sir Lewis Namier, in revenge for some imagined slight? If so, it is just as well that it is posthumous: otherwise what devastating justice it would have received! There would have been no nonsense then about "impeccable logic" in the *Times Literary Supplement!* Or is it, as Mr. Taylor's friends prefer to believe, mere characteristic *gaminerie,* the love of firing squibs and laying banana-skins to disconcert the grav-

ity and upset the balance of the orthodox? Or does Mr. Taylor perhaps suppose that such a re-interpretation of the past will enable us better to face the problems of the present? Theoretically this should not be his motive, for not only does Mr. Taylor, in this book, frequently tell us that the past has never pointed the course of the future, but he has also assured us recently, in the *Sunday Express,* that the study of history can teach nothing, not even general understanding: its sole purpose, he says, is to amuse; and it would therefore seem to have no more right to a place in education than the blowing of soap-bubbles or other forms of innocent recreation. It may therefore be that Mr. Taylor merely means to amuse, not to instruct, by his irresponsible antics. Nevertheless, Mr. Taylor is not noted for consistency and it may be that, in this instance, he does see a connection between the past and the present, a lesson for our times. At any rate, it may be worth while to point out lessons which might logically be deduced from Mr. Taylor's version of history, if it were accepted as uncritically by the public as it has been by their guides, the weekly reviewers.

Basically, the problem is that of the outbreak of world wars. According to Mr. Taylor, the second World War had a double origin: first, it was "implicit" in the general situation; secondly, it was made explicit by the particular blunders of statesmen in the face of that situation. The general situation was created in 1918 when the victorious Allies did not carve Germany up, and so made the ultimate recovery of its "natural weight" inevitable. The particular blunders lay in the failure of Western statesmen to draw the logical conclusions and yield to the inevitable. If only they had shown "realism" and yielded to all Hitler's demands, they would have found them limited and reasonable: it was only war and victory which surprised him by the size of his winnings and made him think of world-conquest.

Now let us transfer these doctrines from the 1930's to the 1950's. The inference is clear. First, the victorious Allies in 1945 did (however unintentionally) carve Germany up, and so (if they will only keep it divided) their settlement of the German problem is "morally valid," and no new German aggression is to be feared. Secondly, in the new circumstances thus created, "realism" consists in allowing the new great power which has replaced Germany in Europe to assert its "natural weight."

Mr. Khrushchev, we should recognise, has no more ambitions of world-conquest than Hitler. He is a traditional Russian statesman of limited aims, and "the moral line" consists in letting him have his way more completely than we let Hitler have his: in other words, unilateral disarmament. Perhaps in this one respect Mr. Taylor does display "methodical and impeccable logic."

DID HITLER HAVE A DESIGN?

ADOLF HITLER
(1928)

The author of this reading needs no introduction; the book from which it is taken does. In 1928 Hitler dictated a manuscript that was revised but for some reason not published during the Nazi era. This manuscript was among the millions of German documents captured by the United States Army at the end of World War II and brought to a great depository at Alexandria, Virginia. There it was found by Professor Gerhard L. Weinberg of the University of Michigan and published in Germany in 1961 by him and Professor Hans Rothfels of Tübingen and the Institut für Zeitgeschichte (Institute for Contemporary History) as *Hitlers zweites Buch* ("Hitler's Second Book"). The Hitler manuscript of 1928 is of particular interest in this booklet because it was devoted almost entirely to a discussion of foreign policy. The views expressed are much the same as those Hitler set forth in 1924 in his famous published book, *Mein Kampf* (*My Struggle*), which was cited in the Nuremberg judgment as proof of Nazism's deliberate, aggressive intentions. In his "book" of 1928 Hitler branded as insufficient any foreign policy that aimed merely to undo the Treaty of Versailles and restore Germany's frontiers of 1914. A. J. P. Taylor had not read "Hitler's Second (or Secret) Book" when he wrote his history of *The Origins of the Second World War*. Had he done so, would it likely have changed his interpretations? Was aggressive war inherent in the whole political philosophy of Nazism? How relevant is proof of Hitler's expansionist ambitions in 1924 or 1928 to the question of responsibility for war against Poland in the specific circumstances of 1939?

POLITICS is history in the making. History itself is the presentation of the course of a people's struggle for existence. I deliberately use the phrase "struggle for existence" here because in truth that struggle for daily bread, equally in peace and war, is an eternal battle against thousands upon thousands of resistances just as life itself is an eternal struggle against death. For men know as little why they live as does any other creature of the world. Only life is filled with the longing to preserve itself. The most primitive creature [could not without it][1] knows only the instinct of the self-preservation of its own "I," in creatures standing higher in the scale it is transferred to wife and child, and in those standing still higher to the entire species. While, apparently, man often surrenders his own instinct of self-preservation for the sake of the species, in truth he nevertheless serves it to the highest degree. For not seldom the preservation of the life of a whole people, and with this of the individual, lies only in this renunciation by the individual. Hence the sudden courage of a mother in the defense of her young and the heroism

---

[1] Words in brackets appeared in the original manuscript but were crossed out in favor of the revised wording as given herein. [Editor's Note]

From *Hitler's Secret Book*, introduction by Telford Taylor, trans. by Salvator Attanasio (New York, 1962), pp. 5–6, 7, 44–45, 88, 139, 142–145, 210. Copyright © 1961 by Grove Press, Inc. Reprinted by permission of Grove Press, Inc.

of a man in the defense of his people. The two powerful life-instincts, hunger and love, correspond to the greatness of the instinct for self-preservation. While the appeasement [fulfillment] of eternal hunger guarantees self-preservation, the satisfaction of love assures the continuance of the race. In truth these two drives are the rulers of life. And even though the fleshless aesthete may lodge a thousand protests against such an assertion, the fact of his own existence is already a refutation of his protest. Nothing that is made of flesh and blood can escape the laws which determined its coming into being. As soon as the human mind believes itself to be superior to them, it destroys that real substance which is the bearer of the mind.

What, however, applies to individual man also applies to nations. A nation is only a multitude of more or less similar individual beings. Its strength lies in the value of the individual beings forming it as such, and in the character and the extent of the sameness of these values. The same laws which determine the life of the individual, and to which he is subject, are therefore also valid for the people.[2] Self-preservation and continuance are the great urges underlying all action, as long as such a body can still claim to be healthy. Therefore, even the consequences of these general laws of life will be similar among peoples, as they are among individuals.

If for every creature on this earth the instinct of self-preservation, in its twin goals of self-maintenance and continuance, exhibits the most elementary power, nevertheless the possibility of satisfaction is limited, so the logical consequence of this is a struggle in all its forms for the possibility of maintaining this life, that is the satisfaction of the instinct for self-preservation.

Countless are the species of all the earth's organisms, unlimited at any moment in individuals is their instinct for self-preserva-

[2] The German word *Volk*, translated here as "people," can also be translated as "nation." It is in this sense that Hitler used the word here and in most cases. [Editor's Note]

tion as well as the longing for continuance, yet the space in which the whole life process takes place is limited. The struggle for existence and continuance in life waged by billions upon billions of organisms takes place on the surface of an exactly measured sphere. The compulsion to engage in the struggle for existence lies in the limitation of the living space; but in the life-struggle for this living space lies also the basis for evolution. . . .

Since history as the representation of the hitherto existing struggles for existence of nations is at the same time the petrified representation of politics prevailing at a given moment, it is the most suitable teacher for our own political activity.

If the highest task of politics is the preservation and the continuance of the life of a people, then this life is the eternal stake with which it fights [consequently the life of a people always stands as the stake], for which and over which this struggle is decided. Hence its task is the preservation of a [that] substance made of flesh and blood. Its success is the making possible of this preservation. Its failure is the destruction, that is the loss of this substance. Consequently, politics is always the leader of the struggle for existence, the guide of the same, its organizer, and its efficacy will, regardless of how man formally designates it, [such a thing] carry with it the decision as to the life or death of a people.

It is necessary to keep this clearly in view because with this the two concepts — a policy of peace or war — immediately sink into nothingness. Since the stake over which politics wrestles is always life itself, the result of failure or success will likewise be the same, regardless of the means with which politics attempts to carry out the struggle for the preservation of the life of a people. A peace policy that fails leads just as directly to the destruction of a people, that is to the extinction of its substance of flesh and blood, as a war policy that miscarries. . . .

In terms of foreign policy the National Socialist movement is distinguished from previous bourgeois parties by, for example, the following: The foreign policy of the national bourgeois world has in truth always been only a border policy; as against that, the policy of the National Socialist movement will always be a territorial one. In its boldest plans, for example, the German bourgeoisie will aspire to the unification of the German nation, but in reality it will finish with a botched-up regulation of the borders.

The National Socialist movement, on the contrary, will always let its foreign policy be determined by the necessity to secure the space necessary to the life of our people. It knows no Germanizing or Teutonizing, as in the case of the national bourgeoisie, but only the spread of its own people. It will never see in the subjugated, so-called Germanized, Czechs or Poles a national, let alone folkish,[3] strengthening, but only the racial weakening of our people. For its national conception is not determined by earlier patriotic ideas of government, but rather by folkish, racial insights. Thus the point of departure of its thinking is wholly different from that of the bourgeois world. Hence much of what seems to the national bourgeoisie like the political success of the past and present, is for us either a failure or the cause of a later misfortune. . . .

The German borders of the year 1914 were borders which presented something incomplete in exactly the same way as the borders of all nations are at all times incomplete. The territorial distribution of the world at any time is the momentary result of a struggle and a development which by no means is concluded, but one which clearly continues further. It is stupid to take the border of any sample year in a nation's history and offhand to represent it as a political aim. We can, of course, present the border of the year 1648 or that of 1312, etc., just as well as the border of the

year 1914. This all the more so as indeed the border of the year 1914 was not satisfactory in a national, military or geopolitical sense. It was only the momentary situation in our people's struggle for existence which has been going on for centuries. And even if the World War had not occurred, this struggle would not have had its end in 1914.

If the German people had in fact achieved the restoration of the borders of the year 1914, the sacrifices of the World War would have been no less in vain. But also, there would not be the slightest gain for our people's future in such a restoration. This purely formal border policy of our national bourgeoisie is just as unsatisfactory in its possible end result as it is intolerably dangerous. Indeed it need not even be covered by the dictum of the art of the possible, for this is above all only a theoretical phrase, which nevertheless seems suitable to destroy every practical possibility.

As a matter of fact such a foreign policy aim also cannot stand up to a real critical examination. Hence attempts are made to motivate it less on logical grounds than on grounds of "national honor.". . .

(For the future an alliance of Germany with Russia has no sense for Germany, neither from the standpoint of sober expediency nor from that of human community.) On the contrary, it is good fortune for the future that this development has taken place in just this way because thereby a spell has been broken which would have prevented us from seeking the goal of German foreign policy there where it solely and exclusively can lie: territory in the East.). . .

I have already dealt with Germany's various foreign policy possibilities in this book. Nevertheless I shall once more briefly present the possible foreign policy goals so that they may yield a basis for the critical examination of the relations of these individual foreign policy aims to those of other European states.

1. Germany can renounce setting a foreign policy goal altogether. This means

[3] The German word translated in this reading as "folkish" can also be translated as "racial" or "racist." This is the meaning intended by Hitler when he used the expression "völkisch." [Editor's Note]

that in reality she can decide for anything and need be committed to nothing at all.

Thus in the future she will continue the policy of the last thirty years, but under other conditions. If now the world consisted just of states with a similar political aimlessness, Germany could at least endure this even though it could hardly be justified. But this is not at all the case. Thus just as in ordinary life a man with a fixed life-goal that he tries to achieve at all events will always be superior to others who live aimlessly, exactly likewise is it in the life of nations. But, above all, this is far from saying that a state without a political goal is in the position to avoid dangers which such a goal may bring in its train. For just as it seems exempt from an active function, in consequence of its own political aimlessness, in its very passiveness it can also just as easily become the victim of the political aims of others. For the action of a state is not only determined by its own will, but also by that of others, with the sole difference that in one case it itself can determine the law of action, whereas in the other case the latter is forced upon it. Not to want a war because of a peaceful sentiment, is far from saying that it can also be avoided. And to avoid a war at any price is far from signifying saving life in the face of death.

Germany's situation in Europe today is such that she is far from allowing herself to hope that she may go forward to a condition of contemplative peace with her own political aimlessness. No such possibility exists for a nation located in the heart of Europe. Either Germany itself tries actively to take part in the shaping of life, or she will be a passive object of the life-shaping activity of other nations. All the sagacity hitherto supposedly able to extricate nations from historical dangers through declarations of a general disinterest has, up to now, always shown itself to be an error as cowardly as it is stupid. Whatever will not be a hammer in history, will be an anvil. In all its development up to now our German people has had a choice only between these

two possibilities. When it itself wanted to make history, and accordingly joyfully and boldly staked all, then it was still the hammer. When it believed that it could renounce the obligations of the struggle for existence it remained, up to now, the anvil on which others fought out their struggle for existence, or it itself served the alien world as nutriment.

Hence, if Germany wants to live she must take the defense of this life upon herself, and even here the best parry is a thrust. Indeed Germany may not hope at all that she can still do something for shaping her own life, if she does not make a strong effort to set a clear foreign policy aim which seems suitable for bringing the German struggle for existence into an intelligent relation to the interests of other nations.

If we do not do this, however, aimlessness on a large scale will cause planlessness in particulars. This planlessness will gradually turn us into a second Poland in Europe. In the very proportion that we let our own forces become weaker, thanks to our general political defeatism, and the only activity of our life is spent in a mere domestic policy, we will sink to being a puppet of historical events whose motive forces spring from the struggle for existence and for their interests waged by other nations.

Moreover, nations which are not able to take clear decisions over their own future and accordingly would like best of all not to participate in the game of world development, will be viewed by all the other players as a spoil-sport and equally hated. Indeed, it can even happen that, on the contrary, the planlessness of individual political actions, grounded in the general foreign policy aimlessness, is regarded as a very shrewd impenetrable game and responded to accordingly. It was this which befell us as a misfortune in the prewar period. The more impenetrable, because they were incomprehensible, were the political decisions of the German governments of that time, the more suspicious they seemed. And all the more, therefore, were especially dangerous ideas suspected behind the most stupid step.

Thus if today Germany no longer makes an effort to arrive at a clear political goal, in practice she renounces all possibilities of a revision of her present fate, without in the least being able to avoid future dangers.

2. Germany desires to effect the sustenance of the German people by peaceful economic means, as up to now. Accordingly even in the future she will participate most decisively in world industry, export and trade. Thus she will again want a great merchant fleet, she will want coaling stations and bases in other parts of the world and finally she wants not only international sales markets, but also her own sources of raw material if possible in the form of colonies. In the future such a development will necessarily have to be protected especially by maritime means of power.

This whole political goal for the future is a utopia, unless England is seen as defeated beforehand. It establishes anew all the causes which in 1914 resulted in the World War. Any attempt by Germany to renew her past along this way must end with England's mortal enmity, alongside which France may be reckoned as a most certain partner from the outset.

From a folkish standpoint, setting this foreign policy aim is calamitous, and it is madness from the point of view of power politics.

3. Germany establishes the restoration of the borders of the year 1914 as her foreign policy aim.

This goal is insufficient from a national standpoint, unsatisfactory from a military point of view, impossible from a folkish standpoint with its eye on the future, and mad from the viewpoint of its consequences. Thereby even in the future Germany would have the whole coalition of former victors against her in a compact front. In view of our present military position, which with a continuation of the present situation will worsen from year to year, just how we are to restore the old borders is the impenetrable secret of our national-bourgeois and patriotic government politicians.

4. Germany decides to go over to [her future aim] a clear, far-seeing territorial policy. Thereby she abandons all attempts at world-industry and world-trade and instead concentrates all her strength in order, through the allotment of sufficient living space for the next hundred years to our people, also to prescribe a path of life. Since this territory can be only in the East, the obligation to be a naval power also recedes into the background. Germany tries anew to champion her interests through the formation of a decisive power on land.

This aim is equally in keeping with the highest national as well as folkish requirements. It likewise presupposes great military power means for its execution, but does not necessarily bring Germany into conflict with all European great powers. As surely as France here will remain Germany's enemy, just as little does the nature of such a political aim contain a reason for England, and especially for Italy, to maintain the enmity of the World War. . . .

Once our people, however, will have grasped this great geopolitical aim in the East the consequence will not only be clarity regarding German foreign policy but also stability, at least for a humanly predictable time, will make it possible to avoid political insanities like those which ultimately entangled our people in the World War. And then we will also have ultimately overcome the period of this petty daily clamor and of the completely sterile economic and border policy.

Germany then, also domestically, will have to take steps toward the strongest concentration of her means of power. She will have to realize that armies and navies are set up and organized not along romantic lines but according to practical requirements. Then she will automatically select as our greatest task the formation of a superior strong land army since our future as a matter of fact does not lie on the water, but in Europe rather.

Only if we will have completely perceived the meaning of this proposition and put an end to our people's territorial need, in the East and on the largest scale, along the lines of this perception will German economy also cease to be a factor of world unrest which brings a thousand dangers down upon us. It will then at least serve the satisfaction of our domestic needs in their major aspects. A people which no longer needs to shunt off its rising rural generations into the big cities as factory workers, but which instead can settle them as free peasants on their own soil, will open up a domestic sales market to German industry which can gradually remove and exempt it from the frenzied struggle and scramble for the so-called place in the sun in the rest of the world.

It is the foreign policy task of the National Socialist movement to prepare and ultimately to carry out this development. . . .

SUGGESTIONS FOR ADDITIONAL READING

This bibliography must be highly selective. Nothing less than the entire post-1914 history of the world, and especially of Europe, needs to be understood if one is properly to appraise the coming of the Second World War. Pertinent studies are listed in George F. Howe and others (American Historical Association), *Guide to Historical Literature* (Washington, 1961). Articles by historians of many nations presenting new facts or interpretations are summarized in *Historical Abstracts*. These are minimum reference works for those who undertake further study of the origins of the Second World War. A journal of major importance for both articles and bibliography is the *Vierteljahrshefte für Zeitgeschichte*.

It goes without saying that study beyond this book should include the full works from which these readings have been selected. The title pages of the readings provide bibliographical data on these works by the International Military Tribunal; William L. Langer and S. Everett Gleason; the Soviet Information Bureau; Charles Callan Tansill; Henry L. Roberts; L. B. Namier; Raymond J. Sontag, Hermann Mau and Helmut Krausnick; Maurice Baumont; A. J. P. Taylor; and Adolf Hitler; the reading by H. L. Trevor-Roper in this book is complete. Other books mentioned in the Introduction to this book might be consulted: Dwight E. Lee, *Ten Years: The World on the Way to War, 1930–1940* (Boston, 1942); D. F. Fleming, *The Cold War and Its Origins, 1917–1960,* 2 vols. (Garden City, 1961); Ludwig Denne, *Das Danzig-Problem in der deutschen Aussenpolitik, 1934–1939* (Bonn, 1959); Martin Broszat, *Nationalsozialistische Polenpolitik, 1939–1945* (Stuttgart, 1961); Wolfgang Wagner, *Die Entstehung der Oder-Neisse-Linie* . . . (Stuttgart, 1953); Mario Toscano, *Le Origini del patto d'acciaio* (Florence,

1948); Walter Hofer, *Die Entfesselung des Zweiten Weltkrieges: Eine Studie über die internationalen Beziehungen im Sommer 1939,* 2nd ed. (Stuttgart, 1955; there is an English translation); William L. Shirer, *The Rise and Fall of the Third Reich* (New York, 1960; a Crest Book paperback edition was published in 1962 by Fawcett Publishers); David L. Hoggan, *Der erzwungene Krieg: Die Ursachen und Urheber des 2. Weltkrieges* (Tübingen, 1961); and Gerhard L. Weinberg and Hans Rothfels (eds.), *Hitlers zweites Buch* (Munich, 1961). Alan Bullock, *Hitler: A Study in Tyranny* (New York, 1952; revised ed., 1960; also available in paperback) is indispensable. Excellent background is also available in Paul Seabury, *The Wilhelmstrasse* (Berkeley, 1954); John W. Wheeler-Bennett, *The Nemesis of Power: The German Army in Politics, 1918–1945* (New York, 1953); and Burton H. Klein, *Germany's Economic Preparations for War* (Cambridge, Mass., 1959). Much *ex post facto* testimony on 1939 by Hitler can be found in H. R. Trevor-Roper (ed.), *Hitler's Secret Conversations, 1941–1944* (New York, 1953). For a brief bibliography of essential works on National Socialism see John L. Snell (ed.), *The Nazi Revolution: Germany's Guilt or Germany's Fate?* (Boston, 1959), a volume in the same series in which this book is published. For the attitude of the anti-Nazi resistance movement toward Hitler's foreign policy the interested reader might begin by consulting Gerhard Ritter, *The German Resistance: Carl Goerdeler's Struggle against Tyranny* (New York, 1958). An excellent German study of military planning for war is Hans-Adolf Jacobsen, *Fall Gelb: Der Kampf um den deutschen Operationsplan zur Westoffensive 1940* (Wiesbaden, 1957). How the presumed exclusive guilt of Germany for

World War II affected wartime Allied planning for the treatment of postwar Germany can be seen in John L. Snell, *Wartime Origins of the East-West Dilemma over Germany* (New Orleans, 1959). Problems of diplomacy in general are treated in Stephen D. Kertesz and M. A. Fitzsimons (eds.), *Diplomacy in a Changing World* (Notre Dame, 1959).

Among many secondary works that are relevant to a study of the origins of the Second World War, the following may be mentioned: Max Beloff, *The Foreign Policy of Soviet Russia, 1929–1941*, 2 vols. (London, 1947, 1949); John Robert Bengtson, *Nazi War Aims* (Rock Island, Ill., 1962); Raymond L. Buell, *Poland: Key to Europe* (New York, 1939); E. H. Carr, *German-Soviet Relations between the Two World Wars* (Baltimore, 1951); Floyd A. Cave and others, *The Origins and Consequences of World War II* (New York, 1948); Boris Cevlovsky, *Das Münchener Abkommen 1938* (Stuttgart, 1958); Winston S. Churchill, *The Gathering Storm* (Boston, 1948); Charles F. Delzell, *Mussolini's Enemies: The Anti-Fascist Resistance Movement* (Princeton, 1961); W. M. Drzewieniecki, *The German-Polish Frontier* (Chicago, 1959); J. B. Duroselle, *Histoire diplomatique de 1919 à nos jours* (Paris, 1953); Keith Feiling, *The Life of Neville Chamberlain* (London, 1946); G. M. Gathorne-Hardy, *A Short History of International Affairs, 1920–1939*, 4th ed. (London and New York, 1950); Gustav Hilger and A. G. Meyer, *The Incompatible Allies: A Memoir-History of the German-Soviet Relations, 1918–1941* (New York, 1953); W. M. Jordan, *Great Britain, France, and the German Problem, 1918–1939* (London, 1943); Ihor Kamenetsky, *Secret Nazi Plans for Eastern Europe: A Study of Lebensraum Policies* (New York, 1961); S. Konovalov (ed.), *Russo-Polish Relations: An Historical Survey* (Princeton, 1945); Hans Leo Leonhardt, *The Nazi Conquest of Danzig* (Chicago, 1942); John A. Lukacs, *The Great Powers and Eastern Europe* (New York, 1953); Stanis-

law Mackiewick, *Colonel Beck and His Policy* (London, 1944); John Brown Mason, *The Danzig Dilemma* (London, 1946); Ian Macleod, *Neville Chamberlain* (New York, 1962); L. B. Namier, *Diplomatic Prelude, 1938–1939* (London, 1948); L. B. Namier, *In the Nazi Era* (London, 1952); Basil Rauch, *Roosevelt: From Munich to Pearl Harbor* (New York, 1950); Pierre Renouvin, *Les relations internationales, 1914–1945* (Paris, 1949); Edward J. Rozek, *Allied Wartime Diplomacy: A Pattern in Poland* (New York, 1958); Bernadotte E. Schmitt (ed.), *Poland* (Berkeley, 1947); Frederick L. Schumann, *Europe on the Eve: The Crisis of Diplomacy, 1933–1939*, 3rd ed. (New York, 1943); James T. Shotwell and Max Laserson, *Poland and Russia, 1919–1945* (New York, 1945); Albert N. Tarulis, *Soviet Policy toward the Baltic States* (Notre Dame, Ind., 1959); Arnold J. Toynbee and Frank Ashton-Gwatkin (eds.), *The World in March, 1939* (London, 1952), and Arnold J. and Veronica M. Toynbee (eds.), *The Eve of the War* (London, 1958), two volumes in the Survey of International Affairs series of the Royal Institute of International Affairs; F. P. Walters, *History of the League of Nations*, 2 vols. (New York, 1952); Gerhard L. Weinberg, *Germany and the Soviet Union, 1939–41* (Leiden, 1954); John W. Wheeler-Bennett, *Munich: Prologue to Tragedy* (New York, 1948); Elizabeth Wiskemann, *The Rome-Berlin Axis* (New York, 1949); Arnold Wolfers, *France and Great Britain between Two Wars* (New York, 1940). It is of some relevance in determining what Hitler's aims were before September, 1939, to examine the policies he followed in occupied Europe after 1939; for this, consult Arnold J. Toynbee (ed.), *Hitler's Europe* (London, 1955), and Alexander Dallin, *German Rule in Russia, 1941–1945* (New York, 1957). The "standard" Soviet history of diplomacy is V. P. Potemkine (ed.), *Histoire de la diplomatie*, 3 vols. (Paris, 1946–1947). The first 200 pages of the following Soviet publication treat the background of the war in greater detail but in the same manner as *Falsificators of History* (Moscow, 1948) did: *Istorii Velikoi Otechestvennoi Voiny Sovetskogo Soiuza, 1941–1945,* 3 vols. (Moscow, 1961); the work of both Soviet and East German historians is set forth in *Der deutsche Imperialismus und der Zweite Weltkrieg,* Vol. I: *Hauptreferate und Dokumente der Konferenz* (Berlin [East], 1960), being reports presented at a conference of the Kommission der Historiker der DDR und der UdSSR in East Berlin, December 14–19, 1959. For development of United States policy in the 1930's, see Robert A. Divine, *The Illusion of Neutrality* (Chicago, 1962).

The memoirs or published collections of papers by diplomats, generals, officials, party leaders, and others that throw light on the diplomacy of the late 1930's are too numerous to list here in detail. Among them are the books by Otto Abetz, Wladyslaw Anders, Kurt Assmann, Józef Beck, Georges Bonnet, Carl J. Burckhardt, Galeazzo Ciano, Robert Coulondre, Birger Dahlerus, Hans Dieckhoff, Herbert von Dirksen, William E. Dodd (diary edited by Martha Dodd), Anthony Eden, Pierre-Étienne Flandin, André François-Poncet, Grigore Gafencu, Maurice-Gustave Gamelin, Hans Bernd Gisevius, Paul Joseph Goebbels, Raffaele Guariglia, Lord Halifax, Ulrich von Hassell, Maurice Hankey, Nevile Henderson, Fritz Hesse, Samuel Hoare, Friedrich Hossbach, Cordell Hull, Tom Jones, Ivone Kirkpatrick, Peter Kleist, Erich Kordt, Massimo Magistrati, Otto Meissner, Léon Noël, Franz von Papen, J. Paul-Boncour, Hermann Rauschning, Joachim von Ribbentrop, Paul Schmidt, Sir John Simon, Henry L. Stimson, Sir William Strang, Jean Szembek, Robert Vansittart, and Ernst von Weizsäcker. These memoirs, like all others, must be used critically by students of history; so used, they are of great value as historical sources. Biographies of some of these men have also been published. An indispensable work on United States policy is Robert E. Sherwood, *Roosevelt*

and Hopkins: An Intimate History (New York, 1948). See also the second volume of John M. Blum's biography of Henry Morgenthau, Jr.

During the war a number of governments published collections of documents to justify their policy in 1939. These include the following: German Foreign Office, *Documents on the Events Preceding the Outbreak of the War: The Second German White Book* (New York, 1940); German Foreign Office, *Polnische Dokumente zur Vorgeschichte des Krieges,* 1. Folge (Berlin, 1940); the "Polish White Book": *Official Documents Concerning Polish-German and Polish-Soviet Relations, 1933–39* (London, 1939); the "British Blue Book": *Documents Concerning German-Polish Relations and the Outbreak of Hostilities between Great Britain and Germany* (London, 1939); *The French Yellow Book: Diplomatic Documents, 1938–1939* (New York, 1940). After the Cold War began the United States published from records captured in 1945 *Nazi-Soviet Relations, 1939–1941: Documents from the Archives of the German Foreign Office* (Washington, 1948), and the Soviet Union published *Documents and Materials Relating to the Eve of the Second World War,* 2 vols. (Moscow, 1948), consisting of Vol. I: *November 1937–1938* and Vol. II: *The Dirksen Papers, 1938–1939;* later the U.S.S.R. published *New Documents on the History of Munich* (London, 1958), consisting of Czech and some Soviet documents. An unofficial collection of Soviet documents has been made available by Jane Degras (ed.), *Soviet Documents on Foreign Policy,* 3 vols. (London, 1951–1953). A major unofficial publication of 1939 material of many nations is the Royal Institute of International Affairs, *Documents on International Affairs, 1939–1946,* Vol. I (London, 1951).

A source of major importance is the body of documentation compiled at Nuremberg by the International Military Tribunal in 1945–1946. Several libraries have full sets of the materials that were never published. The published material itself is voluminous. See especially *The Trial of the Major War Criminals before the International Military Tribunal, Proceedings and Documents*, 42 vols. (Nuremberg, 1947–1949); *The Trial of German Major War Criminals*, 22 vols. (Washington, 1946–1950); and *Nazi Conspiracy and Aggression*, 10 vols. (Washington, 1946–1948).

On German diplomacy in the 1930's the most important published source is the set produced by the joint efforts of United States, British, and French editors, *Documents on German Foreign Policy, 1918–1945* (Washington, 1948–   ); Series D (1937–1941) is most pertinent to the study of the crisis of 1939. Still being published are the *Documents on British Foreign Policy, 1919–1939*, edited by Rohan Butler and E. L. Woodward (later by J. P. T. Bury); the Third Series (1938–1939) has been completed in 9 vols. The Italian records for 1939 have been published by Mario Toscano (ed.), *I documenti diplomatici italiani*, Eighth Series, Vols. XII–XIII (Rome, 1952). American policy may be followed in the Department of State's multi-volume series, *Foreign Relations of the United States: Diplomatic Papers, 1939*, especially Vol. I (Washington, 1956). Neither France nor the U.S.S.R.

has published its documents on foreign policy between the two world wars.

Students who wish to examine archival material should consult: Gerhard L. Weinberg, Fritz T. Epstein, and others, *Guide to Captured German Documents* (Maxwell Field, Ala., 1952); and Gerhard L. Weinberg, for the American Historical Association (published by the National Archives), *Supplement to the Guide to Captured German Documents* (Washington, 1959). Also indispensable are the lists published by the United States National Archives, *Guides to German Records Microfilmed at Alexandria, Va.* Copies of the guides and microfilm copies of the documents they list may be purchased from the National Archives.

New documentary materials continue to appear in the *Vierteljahrshefte für Zeitgeschichte* (Tübingen), 1949–   , which also publishes articles and has an excellent bibliography. See also the guides to doctoral dissertations for various nations, especially: Alfred Milatz and Thilo Vogelsang (eds.), *Hochschulschriften zur neueren deutschen Geschichte*, 1st ed.: *1945–1955* (Bonn, 1956); and the American Historical Association's *List of Doctoral Dissertations in History in Progress or Completed at Colleges and Universities in the United States since 1958* (Washington, 1961), and other lists in this series.